AKSEL SANDEMOSE

AKSEL SANDEMOSE

———————— *Exile in Search of a Home*

RANDI BIRN

———————— Contributions to the Study of World Literature, Number 2

Greenwood Press
Westport, Connecticut • London, England

Library of Congress Cataloging in Publication Data

Birn, Randi.
  Aksel Sandemose : exile in search of a home.

  (Contributions to the study of world literature,
ISSN 0738-9345 ; no. 2)
  Bibliography: p.
  Includes index.
  1. Sandemose, Aksel, 1899-1965—Biography.
2. Authors, Norwegian—20th century—Biography.
I. Title. II. Series.
PT8950.S23Z58 1984   839.8'2372   83-13034
ISBN 0-313-24163-5 (lib. bdg.)

Library of Congress Catalog Card Number: 83-13034
ISBN: 0-313-24163-5
ISSN: 0738-9345

First published in 1984

Greenwood Press
A division of Congressional Information Service, Inc.
88 Post Road West, Westport, Connecticut 06881

Printed in the United States of America

10 9 8 7 6 5 4 3 2 1

In Memory of my Parents
Solveig and Didrik Ingebrigtsen

Contents

Preface

Ever since the publication of <u>A Fugitive Crosses His Tracks</u> in 1933, Aksel Sandemose has been considered a major Norwegian writer. The novel elucidates Sandemose's central theme, that social repression stunts the natural growth of the child and creates violent, miserable adults, unable to relate to the world or to each other. A damaged self-image frequently causes Sandemose's protagonists to avenge themselves upon others in order to cover up their lack of self-esteem. They turn into "werewolves," human beings who "lust for the flesh of other humans or animals."[1]

While Sandemose's characters may at times show physical traits which link them to wolves or other beasts--fangs, claws, paws--they are not genuinely shape-changers. They have more in common with Hermann Hesse's <u>Steppenwolf</u> than with Guy Endore's <u>The Werewolf of Paris</u> or Robert Louis Stevenson's <u>Dr. Jekyll and Mr. Hyde</u>. However, for Hesse the surfacing of the "wolf" side is a necessary first step away from the purely conventional individual towards a true human being characterized by self-knowledge and self-humor. In Sandemose's work the "wolf" represents the incomprehensible, chaotic forces within the psyche which are repressed by conventional society, most notably sexuality. These primitive instincts are not in themselves destructive, and in an ideal social setting they would form an integral part of the total human being. When repressed, however, they tend to grow out of proportion only to explode in violence, war, rape, and other types of anti-social behavior.

Most of Sandemose's protagonists are proletarians, and the author describes the life of small-town workers in early twentieth-century Denmark as a living hell. It is an environment from which the protagonist will at any cost attempt to escape, but to which he is at the same time curiously tied. Sandemose's work can be read as a desperate quest for alternative life styles, different modes of

living which will permit the child to grow into a happy, healthy
adult. In the early stories and novels the sea frequently provides
an outlet, but often life on board turns out to be even more
restrictive than the town from which the sailor has fled. Several
works are situated in far-away lands, Labrador, Newfoundland, and
particularly the Western Canadian prairie. In the New World the
protagonist is seeking new experiences and new opportunities;
perhaps a society radically different from the one he has left
behind can be constructed there? Most often, however, he will discover that the immigrants have brought along in their baggage their
old-world prejudices, social customs, and limited visions. All
they want to do is rebuild the structures they had left behind.

Marriage presents itself as an attractive solution to
Sandemose's early protagonists, especially if, through marital
union they are able to join a more privileged social class. For
marriage to work, however, the protagonist needs to form a union
with an "ideal," self-sacrificing woman, an individual who is
willing and able to extinguish her own needs in order to dedicate
herself to those of the man she loves. Such women become more rare
in Sandemose's later works, and, obversely, sexuality becomes a
fascinating threat from which the protagonist can only obtain protection by escaping into his self. Instead of discovering an outlet in the real world, he starts seeking salvation through artistic
expression.

The Sandemose narrator's ardent desire to escape "Jante," the
synonym for restrictive, conventional society, lends him to a utopian quest for new modes of communal life. This quest culminates
in The Werewolf,[2] where Sandemose appears to have passed the
responsibility for social change to the female heroine, Felicia
Venhaug. Felicia is a powerful, erotic woman with both a daring
social vision and a practical ability to transform her dream into
reality. Felicia is so far ahead of her time that the male
protagonist, Erling Vik, who is strongly attracted to her,
nevertheless feels threatened by her forcefulness. It is only
after Felicia's death that Erling is able to accept her fully and
dedicate the rest of his career as a writer to propagating her
vision. In his attempt to create a more humane society, Sandemose
will frequently uproot his protagonists and place them in
artificial, experimental environments—the frozen plains of
Labrador, a Danish settlement in the New World, a ship at sea, a
tropical island, a greenhouse on a highly unconventional farm.

Sandemose does not believe in a return to nature, and each of
his experimental communities requires very clear laws in order to
function. Once these laws are broken the social order collapses.

While I shall attempt to follow Sandemose's evolution as a
writer from Tales from Labrador through The Werewolf, my focus will
be on the works published since he moved to Norway in 1930. I
shall emphasize the narrator's multiple attempts to free himself
from the bitterness of childhood, and his efforts to carve out for

himself a niche in what he most frequently experiences as a hostile
world. Since women and sexuality play major roles in Sandemose's
work, I shall point out the often conflicting images of women and
the narrator's changing attitude towards sexuality. To attempt a
synthetic reading of Sandemose's work is not an easy task, since
the novels are often extremely complex and the narrator's quest
takes many different forms. My study does not discuss all of
Sandemose's works. Instead I have concentrated on the ones which I
believe illuminate the various stages in his artistic and philosophical development most clearly.

Sandemose is an intensely personal writer. His work has nevertheless been compared to that of Johannes V. Jensen, Jack London,
and Joseph Conrad. In Horns for Our Adornment he reminds us of the
French existentialists in his emphasis on choice rather than submission to a destiny. The similarity, however, can probably not be
carried too far. His chief sources of inspiration were Vilhelm
Grønbech's Vor Folkeæt i Oldtiden; the Icelandic family saga; the
Bible; and Germanic mythology, especially myths related to the sea.
The legends of the "Flying Dutchman" and the "Klabautermann" run
through his whole work. The myths of the werewolf, of Thor with
the thunderbolt, and of the eating of the apple in the Garden of
Eden, are equally significant. Since the late 1920s the works of
Freud and psychoanalysis influenced Sandemose deeply.

A considerable amount of excellent criticism of Sandemose's
work already exists. I especially wish to mention Johannes Væth's
groundbreaking bibliographical and biographical work, Carl-Eric
Nordberg's fascinating biography, Jorunn Hareide Aarbakke's exhaus-
tive study of dreams and visions in Sandemose's fiction, and Asmund
Lien's series of incisive articles, especially on The Past Is a
Dream and the Felicia books. My own study is deeply indebted to the
work of these critics.

I wish to thank Leif Sjøberg for his constant encouragement,
Virpi Zuck for her useful insights, Jorunn Hareide for helping me
complete the bibliography, and Raymond Birn for his untiring support
and excellent advice, especially on style. The work was supported
by a grant from The American Philosophical Society.

Notes

1.   Sabine Baring-Gould, <u>The Book of Werewolves</u>.   New York:
Causeway Books, 1973, p. vii.   This book was originally published
in 1865.

2.   I have used Gustaf Lannestock's translation of <u>The Werewolf</u>.
All the other translations from Sandemose's works are my own.

Chronology

1899 – Aksel Sandemose was born March 19 in Nykøbing Mors, Denmark.

1914 – "Staby vinterlærerseminar."

1916 – Sandemose goes to sea. Jumps ship at Fogo and works in a lumber camp in Newfoundland.

1917 – Returns to sea, then back to Nykøbing.

1919 – Attended "Døckers Kursus" in Copenhagen.

1921 – Completed several novels and plays, all turned down by the publisher. A prose sketch, "Hjemløse fugle" ("Homeless Birds") was published. Contributor to the periodical Scandia. Married Dagmar Ditlevsen.

1922 – Twin girls were born, and shortly after a son was added to the family. A novella, "Den blinde gade" ("The Blind Alley") was published in Johannes V. Jensen's periodical, Forum.

1923 – Fortællinger fra Labrador (Tales from Labrador).

1924 – Ungdomssynd (Sin of Youth), Storme ved Jævndøgn (Storms at Equinox), and Mænd fra Atlanteren (Men from the Atlantic).

1924-25 – Worked as a guard at the Glyptoteket museum, Copenhagen.

1925 – Editor of Hareskov Grundejerblad.

1926 – Death of Sandemose's mother.

1927 - Went to Canada as a correspondent for <u>Berlingske Tidene</u>.
Agricultural worker in Saskatchewan. <u>Klabavtermanden</u> (<u>The</u>
<u>Klabautermann</u>).

1928 - <u>Ross Dane</u>. Sandemose's father died.

1930 - Settled in Norway.

1931 - <u>En sjømann går i land</u> (<u>A Sailor Goes Ashore</u>).

1932 - <u>En flyktning krysser sitt spor</u> (<u>A Fugitive Crosses His</u>
<u>Tracks</u>) turned down by Gyldendal (Oslo).

1933 - <u>En flyktning krysser sitt spor. Fortelling om en morders</u>
<u>barndom</u> (<u>A Fugitive Crosses his Tracks. The Story of a Murderer's</u>
<u>Childhood</u>) published by Tidens Forlag.

1936 - <u>Vi pynter oss med Horn</u> (<u>Horns for Our Adornment</u>).

1937 - <u>Der stod en benk i haven</u> (<u>There Stood a Bench in the</u>
<u>Garden</u>).

1938 - Voyage to Newfoundland and the West Indies. <u>Brudulje</u>
(<u>Brawl</u>).

1939 - <u>September</u>.

1940 - <u>Fortellinger fra andre tider</u> (<u>Stories from Other Times</u>).
German occupation.

1941 - Sandemose fled to Sweden.

1944 - <u>Det svundne er en drøm</u> (<u>The Past Is a Dream</u>) completed.
Sandemose divorced his first wife and married Eva Borgen.

1945 - The couple settled at Kjørkelvik, Norway. Twin sons were
born. <u>Tjærehandleren</u> (<u>The Tar Dealer</u>).

1946 - <u>Det svundne er en drøm</u> published.

1949 - <u>Alice Atkinson og hennes elskere</u> (<u>Alice Atkinson and Her</u>
<u>Lovers</u>).

1950 - <u>Eventyret om kong Rhascall den syttendes tid og om en</u>
<u>palmegrønn øy</u> (<u>Fairy Tale about the Time of King Rhascall the</u>
<u>Seventeenth and about a Palm Green Island</u>).

1951-55 - Sandemose wrote and edited the periodical <u>Årstidene</u> (<u>The</u>
<u>Seasons</u>). From 1952 he received a writer's salary from the
Norwegian government.

1955 - One of the twins died. <u>En flyktning krysser sitt spor.</u>
<u>Espen Arnakkes kommentarer til Janteloven</u> (<u>A Fugitive Crosses His</u>

Tracks. Espen Arnakke's Commentaries upon the Jante Law). Revised
edition of the 1933 novel.

1958 - Varulven (The Werewolf).

1959 - Eva Sandemose died.

1960 - Murene rundt Jeriko (The Walls around Jericho).

1961 - Felicias bryllup (Felicia's Wedding).

1962 - Sandemose married Hanne Holbæk.

1963 - Mytteriet på barken Zuidersee (Mutiny on the Schooner
Zuidersee), a reworking of Ungdomssynd (1924).

1965 - Sandemose died on 6 August in Copenhagen.

---

*In the text I shall refer to Sandemose's works by their English
titles.

AKSEL SANDEMOSE

1.
Biographical Sketch

For most writers childhood is associated with warmth and security; it is an era of intense emotions and proximity to the surrounding world of humans and nature. For Proust's Marcel, childhood was a lost Eden that could only be recaptured through
involuntary memory and art. For Johan Borgen's protagonists it was
"the place" from which they had once been expelled and must conse-
crate a lifetime to regain. By way of contrast, in Sandemose's
work the memories of childhood happiness have been almost completely blotted out by grey, bitter memories of poverty and
exploitation, where the child's growth was systematically stunted
and its self-confidence destroyed.

Accepting the fact that to forget was impossible,[1] Sandemose
would instead confront the problem outright in his work. A Fugitive Crosses His Tracks (1933) is one of the most venomous accounts
of childhood ever written. It is in this novel that Sandemose sets
down the "ten commandments" of his celebrated Jante Law:

1. You shall not believe that you _are_ something.
2. You shall not believe that you are as much as _we_ are.
3. You shall not believe that you are wiser than _we_ are.
4. You shall not imagine that you are better than _we_ are.
5. You shall not believe that you know more than _we_ do.
6. You shall not believe that you are more than _we_ are.
7. You shall not believe that _you_ are good for anything.
8. You shall not laugh at _us_.
9. You shall not believe that anybody cares for _you_.
10. You shall not believe that you can teach _us_ anything.

The repetitious, negative clauses of the Jante law all serve the same purpose, namely to pit the individual against the collective, you against we. While the Jante law is based on Sandemose's personal experiences of childhood, he believed it to be universally valid, that what he had observed and felt other children living in similar environments would see and feel as well.[2] The inhabitant of Jante is oppressor and oppressed at the same time. Individual growth is discouraged, dreams are ridiculed. The Jante child quickly loses its spontaneity and becomes as petty, cruel, and miserable as the adults. Any sign of revolt is efficiently crushed by scorn and ridicule. Everyone is keeping everyone else down, and all are equally miserable.

The childhood Sandemose describes in his autobiographical articles is clearly related to the one he paints in his fiction. The boy, Axel Nielsen,[3] was born in Nykøbing Mors, on an island off the northern coast of Jutland on March 19, 1899, the eighth in a family of nine children. Aksel's parents were almost stereotypes of good working-class people, wearing themselves to shreds to raise their large family. His father was a socialist blacksmith and model worker. The son of an alcoholic, Jørgen Nielsen was himself a total abstainer, "who in the brandy bottle saw the drink of the devil himself."[4] The son's feelings towards him were ambivalent. On the one hand he refers to him as "the kindest God-Father who has ever had children in his care."[5] On the other hand, the father represented an image of authority from which the budding artist would have to free himself in order to find his own identity.

Sandemose's mother, Amalie Jakobsdatter Nielsen, was from Norway. Like most poor mothers of large families at the turn of the century, Amalie worked long hours to keep the group together as an economic unit. She simply lacked the time to cultivate the close emotional relationship which her sensitive and demanding younger son longed for.[6] In order to make up for this lack of intimacy, Sandemose fantasized about her, turning her into a rebellious spirit related to his own.[7] A series of childhood illnesses may be seen in part as attempts on the boy's part to attract the mother's attention, to become special and privileged in her eyes.

For Sandemose, the traditional large proletarian family in which he grew up was an image of hell. The poverty, lack of space, and shared misery did not create a spirit of solidarity. In an article in Aktuell in 1964, he tells us that the nine Nielsen children were never together at any one time.[8] Moreover, he describes the relationships among the brothers as a perpetual power struggle, where the elder and stronger would relentlessly fight to keep the younger and weaker down. In order to defend themselves, the younger must in turn learn tricks and adapt themselves with appropriate masks.

The effect of this oppressive environment on the child was chilling, and it was to take Sandemose a lifetime to free himself from it. Moreover, the atmosphere at home was reinforced by the

wider society with which the boy came into contact, especially
school and workplace. From the age of nine the Nielsen children
were expected to help support the family, and Aksel worked as an
errand boy, program seller at the local movie theater, and
gardener's helper. While he was recognized as an outstanding student, Aksel equated school with a prison, where the children were
grouped in relation to their parents' social status. Aksel's dream
of becoming an entomologist was firmly discouraged, so, instead of
observing and classifying insects, he would ultimately turn his
glance upon human groups. Through stinging descriptions of their
social functions he obtained ample revenge upon those who had
stunted his childhood.

If childhood had been a difficult period for Aksel, adolescence proved far worse. He was confirmed in the spring of 1914, a
ceremony he believed would initiate him into manhood. His disappointment was keen when he discovered that after the event he continued to be a child, but with new responsibilities and expectations placed upon his shoulders. Moreover, the awakening of
sexuality, and the pressure from his peers to perform sexually,
turned his life into hell. He developed a fear of people, assuaged
only by alcohol. He looked upon women as objects of both scorn and
worship. His parents, who must have seen the handwriting on the
wall, decided to send their confused, gifted son to Staby Vinterlærerseminar to train to become a part-time teacher.

While the curriculum at Staby was elementary, it nevertheless
benefited the future writer. The principal was fascinated by gram-
mar, and through him Aksel developed a passion for language. He
discovered literature as well, especially the works of August
Strindberg. However, Sandemose's commitment to a teaching career
was never strong. Instead, he made the traditional choice of any
boy from Nykøbing who wanted to break out of his environment.
During the spring of 1916, right in the midst of World War I, he
went to sea.

Sandemose hated life at sea. Instead of the personal liberty
he had hoped to find far away from his home town, he discovered an
environment which was even more stifling than the one he had left
behind.[10] There were no books to read, no distractions, no sub-
jects for conversation.[11] In the fall of 1916 he informed his
parents of his decision to return home.[12] During the night of
October 29 he abandoned the schooner "Katrine" which was docking at
Fogo, an island off the northern coast of Newfoundland.

The flight was to stand out as a crisis in Sandemose's life.
In his fiction he refers to Fogo as Misery Harbor, and associates
it with Espen Arnakke's murder of his rival John Wakefield. In
Newfoundland he worked in a lumber camp for a while, then signed on
another ship which took him to Portugal, Spain, and then back north
to the Faroe Islands. He returned to Nykøbing Mors in the late
summer of 1917. Soon he fell in with his old acquaintances and the
town appeared to him as stifling as ever. In 1919 he moved to

Copenhagen and enrolled in "Døckers Kursus," an institute for adults who wanted to prepare for the university entrance examination.

Because for the first time Sandemose started to make friends with people who could stimulate his intellectual curiosity, the move to Copenhagen became a turning point in his life. The students at Døckers discussed art and literature, and Sandemose discovered the poetry of Baudelaire and Sigbjørn Obstfelder.[13] While he had always liked to write, as exemplified by the diary he kept at sea, now, probably for the first time, he thought of becoming a professional artist. He completed several novels and plays, all rejected by publishers. Finally, in 1921 the newspaper Morsø Folkeblad accepted a prose sketch, "Homeless Birds," dealing with a young sailor's homecoming. In the same year Sandemose became a contributor to the periodical Scandia.

In 1921, Sandemose married Dagmar Ditlevsen, and within a short time the couple had three children. The struggling would-be writer found his new responsibility heavy to carry and he returned to Nykøbing Mors in hopes of finding a job there. For a while he tried to sell religious tracts, but without much success.[14] He preferred to spend hours each day writing beneath a tree along his route. He unsuccessfully submitted some poems and an animal fable to the novelist Johannes V. Jensen's recently founded periodical, Forum. However, for 100 crowns Jensen bought Sandemose's novella, "The Blind Alley." Even more importantly, Jensen became a mentor for Sandemose, helping and encouraging his literary undertakings. Upon Jensen's advice Sandemose collected a series of stories he had written about Labrador and submitted them to Gyldendal, the leading publishing house in Denmark. An enthusiastic letter from Jensen accompanied the manuscript, and Tales from Labrador was published in 1923. Sandemose admitted that at the time he wrote the stories he had never been to Labrador, although subsequently he did visit the area. The following year he published two novels and another volume of short stories: Sin of Youth, Storms at Equinox, and Man from the Atlantic, but the critical reception was so negative that he was tempted to give up writing altogether. He took a job as a guard at the Glyptoteket museum in Copenhagen, but after two years he decided to get out at any cost.[15]

He continued writing, and fortunately started to have some luck. Despite the poor critical reception of his work, in 1927 he received his first grant, "Carl Møllers legat," and travelled to Canada as correspondent for the Copenhagen daily, Berlingske Tidene. The Klabautermann (1927), his first successful novel, was published in Denmark; moreover, the Canadian experience inspired him to write Ross Dane (1928), the story of the Beaver Coulee settlement in "sunny Alberta." These two books concluded Sandemose's career as a Danish writer.

Sandemose's mother died in 1926, his father in 1928, and the physical ties to childhood were cut. Exactly at this time he began

working on the books which were to become his first genuinely significant literary contributions, A Sailor Goes Ashore and A Fugitive Crosses His Tracks.

Critics have often classified Sandemose's Danish novels as
escapist, ways by which the author attempted to flee the self-
confrontation that had to be made if he were ever to discover his
literary identity. On the other hand one can argue that in the
1920s Sandemose was too close to his childhood to see it in perspective. For Proust, "the only Paradise is the Paradise that one
has lost," and the French writer was unable to write of Combray as
long as his mother was alive, offering continuity between past and
present. Sandemose's childhood was more Hell than Paradise, but he
too had to sense its absolute disappearance before he could take
stock of what had been. It is interesting that soon after he
started to write the books about Espen Arnakke, he decided to leave
Denmark entirely and settle in Norway. In Sandemose's mind the
change of country meant release from paternal authority and a move
towards an unknown part of his self, associated with the mysterious, inscrutable mother.[16]   Consistent with this pattern, his
Norwegian protagonists will shed the physically masculine image of
his Danish heroes and become more androgynous.

Norway in the 1930s provided Sandemose with opportunities for
literary and political activities. Ever since childhood he had
sympathized with the socialist movement, even while doubting the
ability of the oppressed to work together. In his experience the
miserable all too easily were forced into the service of the
oppressive system. Nevertheless, through Sigurd Hoel and Arnulf
Øverland, he associated with the revolutionary Marxist organization
"Mot Dag" ("Towards Day"). Still he kept at some distance, looking
with skepticism upon the bourgeois radicals who made up the bulk of
the membership.

Sandemose arrived in Norway with the manuscript of a new novel
in his baggage, and A Sailor Goes Ashore appeared in 1931, marking
his debut as a Norwegian writer. The same year he completed the
manuscript for A Fugitive Crosses His Tracks. While Sandemose had
doubts about the significance of his Danish novels (he considered
Ross Dane to be an outright falsification of reality), he was
always confident that A Fugitive was an important book. Consequently, it was a hard blow to him when Gyldendal Norsk Forlag
rejected the manuscript, inviting him instead to publish a
Norwegian translation of The Klabautermann. Fortunately, at precisely this time the editor of the newly established Tidens Forlag
was looking for a promising manuscript. Sandemose offered him A
Fugitive Crosses His Tracks, and with the subtitle, The Story of a
Murderer's Childhood, the novel appeared in 1933 and was enthusias-
tically received.[17]

While working on his following books, Horns for Our Adornment
and There Stood a Bench in the Garden, Sandemose wrote a series of
short articles for the dailies Dagbladet and Tidens Tegn. More

importantly, he started his own periodical, Fesjå (Cattle Show),
which served him as an outlet for anything that came to his mind,
memories of childhood, jealousy, anecdotes galore. Only four of
the twenty-five projected numbers of Fesjå ever appeared.

In spite of the fact that he was now an established writer,
Sandemose experienced a very troubling decade in the 1930s. Twice
he was denied Norwegian citizenship because he purportedly failed
to pay his taxes. After having been proposed for a grant by the
Norwegian writers' association, his application was later rejected
because he was a foreigner.[18] His marriage was collapsing, and he
was living in poverty. When Sandemose had to flee to Sweden in
1941, he left the family behind, and during his exile he obtained a
divorce.

The rise of fascism was of course Europe's most pressing
political problem in the 1930s.[19] Shortly after Hitler's seizure
of power in 1933, Sandemose published an angry, almost prophetic
article in Arbeiderbladet. As he saw it, Nazi Germany was but an
extreme example of the evil he had so pitilessly unmasked in his
descriptions of Jante in A Fugitive Crosses His Tracks. He
considered Quisling's call for a union among Germanic peoples
ridiculous.[20] In an article written much later, but which
expresses views Sandemose already held in the 1930s, he defines the
problem of racism in the following way: "Racial hatred is a question of an inferiority feeling on the part of the persecutors.
They feel so small and unsure in themselves. They must live in the
faith that there are at least some who are inferior to themselves."[21] According to Sandemose, only people whose own growth
and imagination have been seriously stunted would feel a need to
believe in their racial superiority. Modern society is an excellent breeding ground for fascism, because it all too often denies
the individual the right to live and let live.

Sandemose's stay in Sweden was to mark the nadir of his life.
He felt unwelcome there, the world was in chaos, and his own life
was in turmoil. Gradually, however, matters straightened out. In
December 1942 the Norwegian government in exile granted him citizenship, and in 1944 he married a fellow refugee, Eva Borgen. She
was exactly the kind of woman Sandemose needed--calm, harmonious,
intelligent, and unscarred by the corruption of society. Belonging
to a solid professional family, Eva possessed a social background
very different from Sandemose's. It is likely that her acceptance
of the writer was instrumental in diminishing Sandemose's self-
image as a persecuted outsider, a view he already had started to
question at the time he met her. In this regard it is important
that his pre-war novels insist upon society's guilt, while the
manuscript he was working on in Sweden focuses on the protagonist's The Past Is a Dream was very difficult for Sandemose to
write.[22] Nevertheless, after five years of work and four rewrit-
ings, the manuscript was completed in 1944. It was first published
in a Swedish translation, two years later in Norwegian.

Upon returning to Norway, Eva and Aksel Sandemose moved to a
small farm, Kjørkelvik, on the southern coast of Norway. Twin
sons, Espen and Jørgen, born in the fall of 1945, symbolized a
fresh start. At Kjørkelvik Sandemose had the space and peace of
mind needed for reflection and writing. Several novels appeared--
The Tar Dealer in 1945, Alice Atkinson and Her Lovers in 1949, The
Fairy Tale about the Time of King Rhascall the Seventeenth and
about a Palm Green Island in 1950. From 1951 to 1955 he was editor
and sole contributor to the periodical Årstidene (The Seasons), of
which thirteen numbers were to appear. Since the publication was
totally dependent upon subscriptions and Sandemose's readers were
often remiss about paying their dues, financial difficulties were a
perpetual problem.[23] The stress was somewhat alleviated when in
1952 Sandemose learned that he would receive a writer's salary from
the government.

The family at Kjørkelvik suffered its first heavy blow in
1953, when Espen became critically ill with leukemia. He suffered
for sixteen excruciating months before succumbing. After a stay in
Italy, Sandemose and his family returned to Kjørkelvik, and Eva
encouraged her husband to continue writing. He worked on an unfin-
ished autobiography, and on his last significant novel, The Werewolf. The book was published in 1958. The enthusiastic reception
brought Sandemose little comfort, since Eva now became ill with
cancer. She died in 1959.

For Sandemose the next few years signified a coming to terms.
The predominant tone of a new autobiography, The Walls around
Jericho, mostly written during the months following Eva's death, is
one of resigned peace. A desire to continue nevertheless prevailed
over Sandemose's sense of resignation. In 1962 he married Hanne
Holbæk, more than thirty years younger than himself. Hanne moved
to Kjørkelvik with several small children from a previous marriage.
In 1963 the couple travelled to Egypt, and in 1965 Sandemose
accepted an invitation to pay an official visit to his home town,
Nykøbing Mors. The fuss and honor shown him by the organizers had
little appeal. He no longer was the young sailor who had dreamt of
flinging success on his own terms at tormentors who preached medi-
ocrity and conformism. A few months after his homecoming he died,
age 66, in a Copenhagen hospital.

Notes

1. Aksel Sandemose, Minner fra andre dager. Artikler i utvalg ved Petter Larsen og Thorleif Skjævesland. Oslo: H. Aschehoug & Co., 1975, p. 20.

2. See Niels Birger Wamberg (ed.), Sandemoses ansikter. Oslo: Aschehoug & Co., 1969, p. 38.

3. Minner fra andre dager, pp. 70-71. Sandemose early changed the spelling of his first name from Axel to Aksel.

4. Carl-Eric Nordberg, Sandemose. Oslo: H. Aschehoug & Co., 1967, p. 15.

5. Ibid., p. 17.

6. Minner fra andre dager, p. 16.

7. Ibid., p. 21.

8. Ibid., p. 102.

9. Nordberg, p. 30.

10. Minner fra andre dager, p. 129. The claustrophobic environment in Sandemose's early sea stories is reminiscent of the hell Jean-Paul Sartre describes in Huis Clos. Paris: Gallimard, 1947.

11. Minner fra andre dager, p. 129.

12. Johannes Væth, På sporet af Sandemose. Nykøbing Mors: Forfatterforlaget Attika, 1975, p. 32.

13. See Leo Estvad, Aksel Sandemose først i 20'rne. Copenhagen: Carit Andersens forlag, 1967.

14. Aksel Sandemose, Epistler og moralske tanker. I utvalg ved Trygve Hagen. Oslo: H. Aschehoug & Co., p. 31.

15. Minner fra andre dager, p. 165.

16. Sandemoses ansikter, p. 45.

17. Nordberg, p. 114.

18. See Bjarte Birkeland, "Forfattermiljø og nazisme in trettiåra." In Nazismen og norsk litteratur, ed. by Bjarte Birkeland and Stein Uglevik Larsen. Bergen-Oslo-Tromsø: Universitetsforlaget, 1975, p. 23.

19. For a detailed discussion of Sandemose's ideas on nazism, see
Jorunn Hareide Aarbakke, "Dumhetens opprør. Aksel Sandemose og
nazismen." In Nazismen og norsk litteratur, pp. 141-58.

20. Nordberg, p. 146.

21. Epistler og moralske tanker, pp. 131-32. Sandemose's italics.

22. See På sporet af Sandemose, p. 128.

23. See Johan Vogt, Sandemose. Minner, brev, betraktninger.
Oslo: H. Aschehoug & Co., 1973.

2.

The Danish Fiction: Exile and the Dream of a Home

Sandemose's Danish fiction is customarily considered to be of minor importance. The characters are one-dimensioned, frequently lacking psychological depth. The solutions to their problems tend to be conventional, either death or integration into the social mainstream through marriage and the founding of a community. Most often the setting is either a sailing ship at sea or North America--Labrador, Newfoundland, the plains of Canada. Sandemose's early protagonists are either sailors or immigrants, people who for various reasons have left their country of origin behind. They are exiles or outcasts in search of a new homeland, which they frequently find by the help of a female savior figure.

Above all, Sandemose's protagonists are on the defensive, ever ready to protect themselves against other people. The author compares these individuals to Thor, the Norse god whose reign ended with the triumph of Christianity. The mythological Thor was a benefactor of humanity in its struggle against the perverse race of giants and the serpent Jørmundgand, symbol of the evil surrounding the world. For Sandemose, however, Thor symbolizes the collective fate of the Norse gods whose primitive rule was overwhelmed by the civilized prohibitions of the Bible, most notably the law of Moses and the theology of Paul. In Sandemose's interpretation of the myth, Thor, once expelled from his seat of power, turned his awesome strength against the human race rather than against its enemies, wielding his hammer in anger and frustration because he had been denied the love and reassurance he believed to be his just due. Interestingly enough, in Sandemose's work the word hammer is linked not only to the author's interpretation of the Thor myth, but also to that of the werewolf, whose ravenous appetite devours the living and dead, humans and animals. According to Montague

Summers, the old Norse term for the transformation of human into animal was skipta hømum and the term for the wolf-shirt which had to be donned for the metamorphosis to be affected was ulfahamr.[1] The phonetic similarities between the Old Norse word hamarr (hammer, Thor's symbol) and hamr (mantle, shirt, associated with the werewolf) may have been sufficient to create in Sandemose's mind the link between the two myths.

Sandemose's protagonists tend to be "hammer men," frustrated individuals carrying deadly weapons, thus presenting a danger both to themselves and others. The crucial question thus becomes: how can a hammer be turned into a tool, an instrument of construction rather than destruction? The two most important protagonists in[2] Sandemose's early fiction are Ross Dane and the "Klabautermann." Ross is the epitome of success, the builder not only of his own farm, but the founder of a whole community as well. He is the obverse of the "Klabautermann," the outcast whose desperate efforts to build a nest for himself all end in miserable failure. In the 1920s Sandemose most likely experienced himself as a failure, an outcast from the human community; yet he wanted to be at its center, the focal point of love and admiration. The fiction clearly reflects the split between psychological reality and fantasy, between the "Klabautermann" and "Ross Dane." In Årstidene Sandemose explained: "It appeared to me that I wanted to write only for myself and about myself, and the 'story' which might come into being was to tell me something I didn't know."[3]

In his early stories Sandemose for the first time develops certain ideas which were to become central to his work, specifically the concept of "the man of luck" ("lykkemannen") and "the man without luck" ("nidingen"). In his book Vor Folkeæt i Oldtiden the cultural historian Vilhelm Grønbech had developed the idea of these two contrasting character types frequently encountered in the Icelandic saga.[4] Sandemose read Grønbech's work in the 1920s. According to Carl-Eric Nordberg, "the man of luck is the one who has the privilege to belong to a family--to feel at home within its closed world," while "the man without luck on the other hand is the one who is forced out of the fortress of security."[5] In Laxdæla saga Kjartan belongs to an aristocratic family endowed with "gipta or hamingja, two Icelandic words for the 'good fortune' or 'success' which is given to a family or to an individual. (The word gipta is etymologically related to the verb to give and therefore refers to something that has been allotted to one.)"[6] According to Peter Hallberg this good fortune is never constant. A "lykkemann" can become a "niding" and vice-versa.

The central theme in The Klabautermann is the outsider's desperate attempt to become an insider, comforted by home and family. It is a book about frustrated male sexuality. Woman is an object of worship. To pull her down from the pedestal is sacrilege punished by death or a fate even worse than death, namely permanent exile from the human community. In the Indian society that Sandemose described in Tales from Labrador the problem was approached pragmatically, and woman was an object that could be bought or sold; in Storms at Equinox the author advocated social integration through love and marriage. In The Klabautermann neither solution applies, and a tone of anguish and despair prevails throughout the book. In view of the author's subsequent Norwegian novels, which all deal with anxiety-ridden protagonists, it is easy to speculate that in books such as Storms at Equinox and later Ross Dane Sandemose was indeed suppressing a side of his self with which he was at the time unwilling or unable to cope. He wanted to be a "man of luck," saved from the self-destructive side of his personality through the intervention of female love and caring. However, he probably had serious reservations about the authenticity of his vision, and these reservations find their expression in The Klabautermann.

The plot in The Klabautermann is suggested by Shakespeare's The Tempest. First there is the name "Ariel," which Captain Klinte has given to his boat. The name symbolizes Klinte's dream of light, love, and beauty. Adam Klinte is a combination of Prospero, the exiled duke of Milan, and Caliban, his scheming, brutal servant. Anna, the young woman he brings onto his ship against her will, is Miranda, whom Caliban attempts to ravish. The Finnish sailor Gösta Porajärvi is the young Alonso, whom Miranda loves. Since, in Sandemose's story, Prospero and Caliban are welded into one character, it is consistent with the Shakespearean analogy that Klinte should in fact abduct and rape his own adoptive daughter. In The Tempest no rape takes place, Caliban abandons his plan and is forgiven by the duke, who in the end endorses the marriage between Miranda and Alonso. In The Klabautermann the "Ariel" sinks, the lovers die, and Klinte is condemned to eternal exile, forever roaming the oceans in search of a home. Sandemose, therefore, has transformed Shakespeare's gentle fantasy into a bitter statement, where evil triumphs over good, and where the dream of love and beauty, when transformed into reality, becomes a weapon of terror and destruction.

Ross Dane was published in Copenhagen in 1928. Retrospectively, Sandemose's attitude towards the novel was negative. He considered it to have represented a pandering to conventional ideas and an apology for the status quo. Nevertheless, the author did reprint the novel in the 1955 Norwegian edition of his selected works, changing the title from Ross Dane to Nybyggere i Alberta (Settlers in Alberta). The title underscores a switch in focus away from the protagonist, Ross, to the community of Danish settlers on the Canadian prairie. Ross Dane is the story of the creation of a predominantly Danish settlement in Alberta at the beginning of the twentieth century. The novel describes the voyage of a group of immigrants from Montreal to Beaver Coulee, thousands of miles to the west, the staking of the land, and the growth of a prosperous farming community. The central theme is the struggle between untamed, violent forces, destructive and death-oriented, and civilizing, life-affirming ones. In Ross Dane the confrontation takes many forms. On one level there is the struggle between

the settlers and the untamed prairie; on another level there is a
constant struggle against the spirit of defeat and psychological
anguish within certain characters. In Sandemose's later works,
combat becomes nearly wholly internalized, analyses of tortured
individuals struggling against death-oriented, primitive forces
within themselves. Though this development can be observed in Ross
Dane, the emphasis of the book is on external enemies, which Ross,
the protagonist, gradually conquers and neutralizes. At the
novel's conclusion harmony reigns in Beaver Coulee, symbolized by
the communal decision to finance the construction of a village
church.

All of Sandemose's works from the 1920s have male protagonists
who are longing for integration within a human community. Conjugal
love is experienced as a road to happiness, and in most cases women
are willing and faithful guides for the men who love them. Mutual
love or a practical, mutually satisfying agreement, as suggested in
some of the stories in Tales from Labrador, are seen as a positive
basis for a happy union, while sexual violence leads to chaos and
death. Sandemose's early protagonists wish to be builders, but
their ambition seldom goes beyond the desire to construct a secure
nest for themselves and their loved ones. The notable exception,
of course, is Ross Dane, who wishes to transform the Canadian prairie into a prosperous farming community. The community Ross would
like to see in Beaver Coulee is peaceful, built upon generosity and
compassion rather than jealousy and greed. For Ross, human qualities are more important than racial or ethnic ties. Far from being
a utopian dreamer, Ross himself is practical and down-to-earth. He
sees honesty, hard work, and humility as the road to a happy, harmonious life. While the inhabitants of Beaver Coulee very frequently display selfishness, greed, and prejudice, one has the
feeling that in the end good will prevail over evil. In
Sandemose's next two novels, A Sailor Goes Ashore and A Fugitive
Crosses His Tracks, the picture has become more complex. The protagonist's past has become a determining factor, adding a psychological depth which was lacking in the works from the 1920s.
Moreover, on the interpersonal level, the reader now perceives the
narrator's willingness to explore unconventional paths towards
human happiness.

Notes

1. Montague Summers, <u>The Werewolf</u>. New York: University Books, Inc., 1966, p. 242.

2. A thorough study of the myth of the Klabautermann has been made by Reinhard F. Buss in his monograph, <u>The Klabautermann of the Northern Seas</u>. Berkeley, Los Angeles, London: University of California Press, 1973. Buss confirms the association between the Klabautermann and Thor. See <u>The Klabautermann of the Northern Seas</u>, p. 110. There is nothing in Norse mythology, however, to substantiate Sandemose's view of Thor as an unhappy outcast. Thor is normally portrayed as a boisterous giant, probably the most popular of the Norse gods. It is likely that Sandemose made the link between Thor and the Klabautermann because they were both traditionally associated with hammers. See <u>The Klabautermann of the Northern Seas</u>, p. 12. In Sandemose's works names derived from Thor (Tor, Torson) and <u>hammer</u> (Hamre) have an unhappy connotation.

3. <u>Årstidene</u>, 3 (1952), p. 9.

4. <u>På sporet af Sandemose</u>, p. 66. See P. M. Mitchell, <u>Vilhelm Grønbech</u>. Boston: Twayne, 1978, pp. 24-29.

5. Nordberg, p. 69.

6. Peter Hallberg, <u>The Icelandic Saga</u>, translated with Introduction and Notes by Paul Schach. Lincoln: University of Nebraska Press, 1962, p. 89.

3.

A Sailor Goes Ashore:
Arrival at Point 0

Describing the second generation of settlers in Beaver Coulee, A Sailor Goes Ashore can be considered a sequel to Ross Dane. Ross has become an old man, who has voluntarily stepped down from his throne, and the focus shifts to a younger group of immigrants, most notably Espen Arnakke, Sten and Maja Eriksen, and the Bodilsen sisters, Kristine and Gjatrid. Ross's personal and psychological problems occupied a relatively minor role in the novel concerned with his development. On the other hand, Espen Arnakke, the protagonist of A Sailor Goes Ashore, is mainly concerned with putting his own life in order. Having murdered a man shortly after jumping ship in Newfoundland, he arrives in Beaver Coulee as a fugitive from the law. In a deeper sense, he also is a fugitive from an inner conflict which he has been unable to confront and resolve. The novel shows how Espen, through a meeting with social values different from his own and through exposure to eroticism and love, manages to find resolution. At the book's conclusion he is ready to marry his fiancee Gjatrid, and settle down as an integrated member of the community.

While Ross Dane was an epic novel, A Sailor Goes Ashore is a psychological one. Between 1928 and 1931 Sandemose became seriously interested in the work of Freud and methods of psycho-analysis, exposures which had a profound impact on his writing.[1] Moreover, it was during the writing of A Sailor Goes Ashore that Sandemose decided to leave Denmark and settle in a new land, Norway.

Arrival at Point 0

The first part of A Sailor Goes Ashore describes Espen's life
at sea. Espen's existence on board the "Rurik" is miserable.
Enduring excruciating pains in his eyes and an ever diminishing
vision, Espen meets only scorn, ridicule, and cruelty from his
superiors and peers alike. The situation reaches its climax when
the captain orders him out of his bunk to fasten a sail, a dangerous job even for a person whose vision is intact. Somehow Espen
performs the task, only to be welcomed afterwards by a string of
blows. As stars begin dancing before his eyes, the sadistic crew
members pull down his trousers to continue the beatings. Realizing
that he has reached a turning point in his life, the masochistic
Espen experiences a sense of joy. After having lost its course in
the storm, the "Rurik" sights land. The inhospitable rocks turn
out to be Deadman's Point in Newfoundland, symbolically the end of
a road and the possibility of a new beginning.

The description of Espen's suffering on the "Rurik" foreshadows the descriptions of Jante in Sandemose's next novel, A
Fugitive Crosses His Tracks. In A Sailor Goes Ashore the protagonist feels martyrized: "He was a saint they were spitting at."[2]
The beatings on the deck mark a climactic moment in Espen's life;
no longer will he suffer injustice on the ship. He has reached
Point 0_3 in his existence: "He would stake his life at Deadman's
Point."[3] He will gamble, jump ship, and either swim to shore or
drown in the waves. In spite of the dark and cold, Espen is filled
with confidence during his long swim: "I am a man of personal
liberty for the first time in my life, now, while swimming across
the ocean towards Deadman's Point. . . I know where I am, I know
who I am, I know everything in the world, I know everything in the
world."[4]

Espen survives his gamble and crawls ashore on a grey, naked
cliff. Unlike Kierkegaard's persona, who, surviving his jump into
the deep, could expect eternal bliss, Espen discovers that Deadman's Point is merely the first step on the long road towards self-
realization.[5] Looking towards the ocean, wet and cold, Espen
notices a bundle drifting in his direction. He first believes
providentially that it is the belongings he had dropped into the
water as he fled the "Rurik": "Blankets, clothes, diaries, pictures, books, tobacco in a can, pipes, sailors' boots--."[6]
Instead, he discovers that the floating object is a corpse. Symbolically, the dead man is a part of Espen himself, the side of his
personality left behind. Espen leaves the corpse on the cliff, but
has neither the time nor the tools to bury it. Consequently, its
ghost will haunt him in his dreams. The entire novel may be read
as Espen's struggle to rid himself of the shadow that he carried
along from the past. Genuine liberation comes only at the conclusion of the novel. Espen's journey will take him from Deadman's
Point to Misery Harbor, Despair Bay, and finally to Ross Dane's
settlement in Beaver Coulee, where he will gradually succeed in
freeing himself from the ghost. Like Erik Skjelholm and Kresten

Ravnsberg, the heroes of Storms at Equinox, he ultimately finds peace through the founding of his home and family.

Misery Harbor and the Confrontation with John Wakefield

At the root of Espen's problem is an inability to live harmoniously with other people. He experiences interpersonal relationships in terms of master and slave, and he sees himself inevitably cast in the inferior position: "A slave he was to be, that was his fate if he ventured too close to other human beings, a slave of people who had nothing but meat and bone in their head."[7] His flight from the "Rurik" had been in revolt against his slave state and against his own slave mentality.[8] "Hereafter he wanted to be his own master."[9] Put another way, Espen wishes to abandon his assigned role as a "man without luck" in order to turn himself into a "man of luck." While vaguely sensing that a mere shifting of roles may not be the real solution to his problem, he is at this point unable to perceive of other options.

Espen's first challenge comes in Misery Harbor, where the tall, handsome John Wakefield becomes his rival for Eva, a young woman with whom both men have fallen in love. The attitudes of John and Espen towards Eva are diametrically opposed. For John, she is a tempting fruit whose flesh he hungers to devour as quickly as possible and spit out the pit. On the other hand Espen, whose sexual experiences have been consistently disappointing, is fearful of touching Eva. He sublimates by placing her on a pedestal where he can worship her from a safe distance: "Then he turned Eva into a saint, wouldn't dream of possessing her, the pure virgin."[10]

Both the attitudes of John and Espen are aberrations, provoked by unhealthy social environments. In Espen's home town, Jante, a young boy's sexual experiences were the measure of manhood. Women were objects and prizes in a nightly game among street-corner adolescents. Since Espen's own "conquests" had never led to the promised bliss, they instilled in him a complex of inferiority and a fear of impotence. In fact, his slave mentality has its source in his relationship to women. While not from Jante, John Wakefield must have grown up in a similar environment.[11] In his case, however, the psychological result was different. He came to look upon himself as a conqueror, and his ego grew in proportion to the number of women he seduced and subsequently rejected. One night in an abandoned house John seduces Eva while Espen listens to the scene from a hideout in the attic. In a subsequent confrontation with Espen, John boasts about his deed and ridicules Espen's lack of virility. In order to prove his point, John embraces Espen and starts fondling his body. Psychologically Espen is now in a state similar to the one in which he found himself while he was being beaten on the deck of the "Rurik." He is the victim of a cruel force bearing down upon him in an attempt to destroy whatever vestige of self-esteem he possesses. Again, this is a turning point, a moment of revolt. He draws his knife and stabs John to death.

The slave suppressed, the "man of luck" in Espen surfaces. Big
John has been reduced to a harmless object: "He was just <u>something</u>
lying there now."[12] It is worth noticing that just before Espen
pulls his knife, he feels a stinging pain in his eyes, again a
parallel to the situation which led him to the flight from the
"Rurik."

The struggle between Espen and John resembles an existentialist confrontation. According to Sartre, individuals are constantly confronting each other in psychological battles, where a
given contestant must play either the dominant or the subordinate
role, master or slave. For Sandemose and Sartre, both roles carry
certain psychological gratifications. Espen does get a measure of
masochistic pleasure from his slave role, and John Wakefield
clearly cherishes his role as sadist. Moreover, on the initiative
of either player the roles can be reversed. If Espen's tormentors
drive him too far, he will revolt in an attempt to render them
harmless and assume the dominant role himself.

Finally, for both Sandemose and Sartre, simple reversal of
roles does not signify genuine change. A more desirable solution
would be to create a personality where the extremes have been neu-
tralized. To be genuinely human is to be neither slave nor
conqueror.[13] Neither Espen nor John was able to relate to other
human beings in general and to women in particular, and this is
basically what Espen must learn to do before he can find his true
identity and settle down to a peaceful life.

Within the framework of the novel, the killing of John
Wakefield is presented in a positive light. While himself a victim
of environment, John nevertheless represents a set of despicable
characteristics: ego-centered sexuality, cruelty, sadism, and a
total disregard for others. John incarnates those forces which had
cast Espen into the slave role. By being rid of John, Espen rids
himself of his submissive side. Symbolically and literally, the
murder of John permits Espen to escape from Misery Harbor and sends
him on his way to the more sanguine environment of Beaver Coulee in
"Sunny Alberta." Far from resolving Espen's psychological problems, however, the murder is only a small step ahead. It results
in a release from the slave mentality, but fails to produce an
integrated personality.

<u>Alternative Life Styles and the Possibility</u>
<u>of a New Society</u>

In Espen's mind the name Beaver Coulee was associated with
success, a Scandinavian kingdom with Ross Dane on the throne.[14] Upon
arriving, however, he finds nothing but "desolate prairie," and
discovers that Ross is merely a lonely, cynical old man who has
long since voluntarily abrogated his power. While many of the old
timers still are there, new people with different values and different backgrounds have moved in: Vilfred Larsen, a Communist

idealist, Sten and Maja Eriksen, a young couple of upper-class
Copenhagen backgrounds, Røde Fane, an inscrutable Dutchman who will
spend most of his time in the local tavern. While Røde Fane's
character is not developed in A Sailor Goes Ashore, he will become
the protagonist in a later Sandemose novel, September, along with
Vera and Emil, who are reincarnations of Sten and Maja.

One of Espen's chief models in Beaver Coulee is Vilfred
Larsen, a farmer and worker who is passionately interested in edu-
cating himself about the structure of society. Heir to the eigh-
teenth-century Enlightenment, Vilfred believes that reason ought to
prevail in all things, and so he rejects both violence and
religion. Above all, Vilfred believes that it is possible for
people to improve their lot. He considers money to be the key
social problem, because society does not have the knowledge or will
to use it for the greatest benefit of all its members: "He would
talk about what a wonderful tool money could be in the hands of the
right power. One day reason would conquer, shatter barbaric
notions about divinities, cut the head off the monster of national-
ism, and take control of the stray money."[15]

While Vilfred is not insensitive to women, most notably to
Maja Eriksen, he refuses to permit passion to prevail over reason,
even in love. At the novel's conclusion Vilfred does found a new
society--on a very small scale, to be sure. On an early spring day
he returns to Beaver Coulee with an adopted son after taking one of
his annual study tours to libraries in the United States. He has
chosen to become a father without confronting the problems of women
and sexual passion. While Espen clearly admires Vilfred and looks
up to him, he never tries to follow his example. With his self-
control, rationality, and unswerving faith in human progress,
Vilfred does not readily fit into Sandemose's fictional world of
self-destructive passions and irrational behavioral patterns.
While he will reappear in September, again as a minor character, he
has little impact on Sandemose's total work, and will disappear
altogether from the later novels.

A more profound influence on Espen are Sten and Maja Eriksen,
a couple with a social background widely different from his own.
Unlike the other settlers, it was not material need or a desire to
escape an intolerable social environment that made Sten undertake
the long journey from Denmark to Alberta. An engineer by profes-
sion, Sten wanted to return to the soil and participate in the
experience of perfect freedom which he associated with the new
world. Sten's utopian idealism will soon have to confront reality,
however. He becomes deeply disappointed when he discovers that the
immigrants were not at all ready for the freedom offered them in
Canada. Instead of working together towards the construction of a
new society, they are busy rebuilding the structures they had left
behind: "It was as if the bottom had fallen out of their souls,
the world had become too big, it threatened to become endless.
They suffered like wild beasts who had had freedom imposed on them
by an animal friend, they looked around bewildered and wanted to
recreate the cage."[16]

The other settlers do not like Sten, whom they consider to be
patronizing and snobbish. They resent his educated, correct
English, polished manners, and what they see as an unorthodox life
style. The novel makes it clear that Sten never intended to break
completely with his heritage when he moved to the New World. He
had naively believed that he could carry along from Denmark whatever he thought to be valuable in his old culture and integrate it
into the new one, thus creating the perfect society: "Sten Eriksen
had brought furniture, paintings, and books from Denmark, his
living quarters were like a piece of bourgeois Copenhagen."[17]   Sten
does not seem to understand that his desire to carry along the past
may be his greatest obstacle on the road towards the future.

The resentment against Sten will be crystallized in a growing
anger against his wife, Maja, who becomes a target of community
gossip. Maja is an exceptionally kind and beautiful woman who
attracts several of the young men in Beaver Coulee. According to
rumor-mongering townsfolk, she has in her time taken many lovers;
and the proper citizens gradually build up a hatred against her
which peaks when a self-appointed delegation arrives at the Eriksen
farm with the intention of forcing the family out of the community.
Sten physically defends himself and his wife, and the "delegation"
is driven away from the farm.

A careful reading of the book makes it clear that Sten's problem may not be the community at all, but rather his emotions
towards Maja. While he likes to believe that he left Copenhagen
for Canada because of a longing for unlimited freedom, there are
indications in the novel that his real reason may have been less
noble. Sten may in fact have wished to remove Maja from Copenhagen
and an old lover, Jens Abildgard. If this reading has any merit,
the controlling element in Sten's character is not utopianism, but
jealousy.

Maja, not Sten, is the truly free individual in Beaver Coulee.
She is the first in a series of intelligent, non-conforming women
in Sandemose's work, a forerunner of Vera in September, Alice in
Alice Atkinson and Her Lovers, and Felicia in The Werewolf. In A
Sailor Goes Ashore Maja's character is not well developed. What we
know of her is based largely on rumors, and on the stories of the
alcoholic Rolf Hansen, who claims to have made love to her in the
Eriksen's barn. Although Espen is clearly attracted to Maja, and
the townspeople believe him to be her lover, there is no evidence
in the book that he ever touches her.

As Sandemose introduces Sten and Maja, their relations are
ambiguous. They sleep in different bedrooms and decided beforehand
how many children they wanted to have. Sten treats Maja with great
respect, listening attentively whenever she speaks, even in the
company of other men. In short, he treats her as his equal in
every way, yet fails to understand her and accept her as she is.
Unlike the later novels, in A Sailor Goes Ashore the problem is
resolved conventionally with Sten reclaiming his relinquished

authority over Maja. Her genuine or imagined lovers are either
humiliated or else forced to sublimate their desire for her. Jens
Abildgard, who unexpectedly shows up on the prairie, is first shot
by the jealous Rolf, then unmasked as a thief and removed from the
community by the police; Vilfred Larsen avoids Maja altogether by
adopting a son and concentrating on male companionship; Espen, as
we shall see later, will turn his attention from Maja towards other
women. The relationship between Sten and Maja concludes with Sten
becoming sexually more assertive towards the end of the book. On
her side Maja accepts her role as monogamous, submissive wife:
"There was something in his [Sten's] voice that scared her. This
was a command, and she had never experienced it before. But now
she had the courage to accept anything. Even to obey."[18] While
Maja remains out of reach of Espen throughout the novel, she does
provide him with a female model. Moreover, Maja's eventual
submission to Sten reestablishes the ideal of a conventional
marriage based on mutual conjugal fidelity.

On the other hand, Sten teaches Espen to face up to his problems, to resolve rather than run away from them. Throughout the
novel, Sten often was tempted to leave Beaver Coulee rather than
fight with the community. In the end, however, he decides to stay:
"He had come here to win. He had burned his ships. I am staying
in Beaver Coulee."[19] Sten's decision echoes the advice Ross Dane
had given Espen on the latter's arrival six years earlier: "Yes,
run away we all know how to do, but remain where we are, be torn to
rags and then put together again in the right way, that is more
difficult."[20] According to Sten, true freedom can be found only by
coming to terms with the environment into which one is born: "One
could find freedom here, by staying on the place where he was born
and freeing himself from siblings, from parents, and from his
social circle, be above them, and love them nevertheless. But
things like that do not happen."[21] Espen interprets Sten's words
as telling him to return to his birthplace, Jante in Denmark, in
order to explore the roots of his misery. He is far from ready to
undertake such a voyage, however. Instead, like Sten, he decides
to build his existence in Beaver Coulee: "It was pure misery that
he never could finish with those things which were left behind in
his path. You ought to get married, Espen, and become good, you
ought to become a builder, have a son and teach him to plough."[22]
The solution will prove to be only tentative. In Sandemose's next
novel Espen will indeed return to Jante. In order genuinely to
free one's self, the fugitive must possess the courage to cross his
own tracks.

The Two Sisters--Eroticism and Love

For Espen, Maja remains a taboo, a goddess to worship but
never touch. For a female partner he will look elsewhere, towards
Old Bodilsen's farm, the home of Kristine and Gjatrid, two of
Bodilsen's daughters.

Espen sees Kristine as strong and beautiful. He is both attracted to her and repelled by her. Two years older than Espen, she is a sexually aggressive woman. It is with her that Espen has his first completely fulfilling erotic experience, occurring wholly by chance in broad daylight in the middle of Jens Abraham's wheat field. While Sandemose does not detail the encounter, Espen's sexual release is obvious: "And he who had been at the point of losing his faith that a woman can be delicious."[23] In the following paragraph we are informed suddenly that Espen has become virtually blind, an ominous reminder of the situation on the "Rurik" several years earlier. Again, then, Espen may be at a crossroads, and will have to choose a direction for his future.

For Espen the relationship with Kristine turns unhappy. In his mind she becomes closely associated with John Wakefield and Misery Harbor. Even before anything has developed between the two, Espen sneaks glances at her in church: "No, he had to peak at Kristine. Her back was breathing. Her bodice was like a triangle standing on its point, she was so big and strong that Espen felt too small again. He was humming the Internationale to himself. John Wakefield, why didn't you measure strength with someone like Kristine instead of with Espen from Jante?"[24]

Kristine makes Espen feel insufficient. She reduces him to the state in which he found himself on the deck of the "Rurik" or when humiliated by John Wakefield in Misery Harbor. Her love returns him to the powerless state of childhood: "She placed her arm around his neck and pulled him towards her:--You are a small child, Espen."[25] Psychologically, therefore, for Espen Kristine becomes the female counterpart of John Wakefield. As on the deck of the "Rurik," Kristine's power awakens in Espen an irresistible desire to revolt: "He was humming the Internationale to himself." If Espen is to survive, he must liberate himself from Kristine.

During his period of blindness, the image of the swim towards Deadman's Point keeps surfacing in Espen's mind. The antagonist waiting on the shore, however, is not John Wakefield, but Kristine: "For a whole week Espen was sitting there in his chair. He was dreaming again and again that he was swimming from the Atlantic towards Deadman's Point. There on the grey coast which was so deserted and silent that one could sit down and cry, Kristine was walking on the beach waiting for him. She held a knife between her teeth. But each time he would drown by the outermost rock and call out for Eva from Misery Harbor."[26] While Espen clearly feels that he needs a woman to help him survive, he cannot cope with Kristine, because she is too strong. In her relationship to him, she is the giver and he is the taker. When working in the fields, Kristine dresses in masculine clothing, and in her eyes Espen perceives a masculine desire to rule. Above all, Kristine hardly needs Espen to take care of her: "What did she need a man for? She could stake out land and run a farm much better without."[27] Kristine even takes on the role of hunter, at one point barely missing Espen with a rifle shot, claiming to have mistaken him for a coyote. For

Kristine, Espen is a prey that she wishes desperately to catch.
Espen, on the other hand, fears Kristine and wishes to be rid of
her, yet to break loose is as difficult for him as for an alcoholic
to turn down the offered bottle: "She was so beautiful! Oh,
Kristine, I love you, you tear me apart, tear me apart like . . .
an enormous glass of brandy,"[28] or "But oh, Kristine, to meet you
is like burning from an unquenchable thirst, that of the ship-
wrecked sailor, the alcoholic, the diabetic, and then have a
two-foot beaker placed before one's mouth."[29]

Espen's reasons for rejecting Kristine are complex. First of
all, his feelings for her are wholly physical, and she does not at
all correspond to the idea he has formed of what a woman ought to
be like. She is freely offering her eroticism, while Espen associates his ideal woman with sexual purity and virginity. Kristine is
active, while Espen believes women ought to be passive. To accept
Kristine would be to permit his passions to prevail over his better
judgment: "It will most likely go the way you do not want," Maja
tells him.[30] This was precisely what had happened to Charles
Villeneuve, the half Indian in Ross Dane. In spite of his firm
decision to marry a white woman and join what he saw as the wave of
the future, Charles let his passions run away with him one night in
Beaver Coulee. He married an Indian woman that his reason
rejected, and as a result never managed to come to terms with his
identity. Because of an inability to control his passions, Charles
never became the builder and farmer he wished to be. Espen wants
to retain his freedom of choice, to decide the direction for his
own life rather than be a victim of irrational physical drives.
Interestingly enough, he does not attempt to free himself of
Kristine by leaving Beaver Coulee. On the contrary, he takes a job
at the Bodilsen farm, where he will be able to confront the problem
head on.

The treatment of Kristine in A Sailor Goes Ashore reveals
Sandemose's horror of the strong, sexually aggressive woman. The
protagonist experiences her as a monster who will reduce him to a
state of total powerlessness. She is, in fact, as damaging to the
healthy development of the male personality as was Jante to the
child; to permit her to get her way would signify spiritual death:
"It was like being pulled off to market, come on now! You are only
going to be slaughtered!"[31] She presents a formidable obstacle
that Espen must conquer on his road to self-identity.

Espen's double attraction towards Kristine and her younger
sister, Gjatrid, corresponds to Charles Villeneuve's simultaneous
pull towards the Indian and the white race. While Charles permits
his passions to prevail, Espen successfully suppresses his sexual
drive towards Kristine. Instead, he focuses his attention on
Gjatrid, who is only fifteen years old when Espen moves to the
Bodilsen farm. Gjatrid is the incarnation of youthful innocence.
One evening when the two are home alone (it is the night of
Kristine's wedding to another man), Gjatrid climbs into Espen's bed
to seek protection from the thunderstorm raging outside. The scene

may be read symbolically if we remember that Sandemose would frequently associate his wayward protagonist with Thor, the Norse thunder god. Espen, however, suppresses his primitive instincts, his Jante morality, which would have led him to take advantage of Gjatrid's innocence. In other words, he suppresses the Thor side of his personality.

Gradually, Gjatrid's love and confidence will help Espen conquer Jante. Above all, she helps him overcome the Jante dogma that one has to prove his virility by sexual conquests and the accompanying downgrading of women. To her he is able to confess his weaknesses and fears without shame, and he learns to scorn the old Jante god: "I have by far outgrown my own ideal and am now able to scorn it. You are an old, collapsed idol, John Wakefield."[32] While Jante had caused Espen to lose all self-confidence, Gjatrid manages to reinstill in him a belief in his own ability: "He accomplished pure miracles just because she believed he was able to."[33]   Sure of possessing her love, he no longer needs to swing his hammer to prove he is strong and powerful. By kindling in him a desire to start building his own house, Gjatrid, in fact, helps Espen turn the hammer into a constructive tool instead of a weapon used to frighten, wound, and even kill others. Finally, Gjatrid brings Espen closer to the point when he can confront Jante head on, return to his childhood, and finally understand why he became the way he is. When he later decides to visit Gjatrid, who has spent several months with relatives in Manitoba, for the first time in his life Espen is able to travel eastward, that is to move back in the direction from which he had come: "You are at the point of dying, John Wakefield, I dare travel towards the east!"[34]

The catalysing moment for Espen comes when he learns that Gjatrid is carrying his child. The news comes in a letter that Espen receives during a Christmas celebration with friends in Beaver Coulee. It is as if an avalanche occurs inside him, ridding him of the frozen shell that Jante had wrapped around his heart: "Oh, there the avalanche of sand and earth and stone cascaded down the mountain side, and there was the mountain after the avalanche, a shining mountain of gold glimmering in the sun. Gjatrid, my darling."[35]   The golden, sunny mountain reflects Espen's feelings about himself. Warm, rich, and beautiful, he is proud to show his feelings to others. The news reaches Espen on Christmas night, confirming that the protagonist has been saved through love and the birth of a child. The immediate consequence of what has happened is that for the first time in his life Espen is able to tell his friends the story of John Wakefield and the shadow it has cast over his life: ". . . and Espen was talking on and on about a most secretive person who crossed Canada on one elbow one night."[36]   The secretive person is, of course, John's ghost, which has haunted Espen ever since he left Misery Harbor six years earlier. It is as well the ghost of the corpse he did not bury before leaving Deadman's Point, it is the Jante side of his own personality. A Sailor Goes Ashore ends on a note of celebration and reconciliation. During the night Espen dreams once again about the swim from the

"Rurik" towards Deadman's Point. This time, however, he is both
mentally and physically a survivor: "That Christmas night Espen
was dreaming once again he was swimming towards Deadman's Point,
but this time he reached shore alive. Kristine was kneeling on the
beach, her hair flowing around her. He closed his eyes as he
lifted the dagger which he had between his teeth: 'Now it is
finished, Kristine!' His voice was deep with triumph. She bent
her head and didn't answer. He killed her on the beach."[37]

The symbolic murder of Kristine, yet another symbol of Jante,
signifies that Espen has completed the liberating process he began
when leaving the deck of the "Rurik," six years earlier. The
flight from the ship and subsequent killing of John Wakefield were
only able to free him partially from his past. The final dream
indicates that Jante has lost its grip upon his mind. His
relationship to others, especially women, will no longer be
controlled by the master/slave principle. The past appears to be a
clean slate, and Espen will be able to bring Gjatrid and the child
into the house he has constructed, thereby turning it into a
genuine home.

Notes

1. See Jorunn Hareide Aarbakke, Høyt på en vinget hest. Oslo: H. Aschehoug and Co., 1976, pp. 40–42; p. 69.

2. Aksel Sandemose, Verker i utvalg, III. Oslo: H. Aschehoug and Co., 1966, p. 160.

3. Ibid.

4. Ibid., p. 163. Sandemose's italics.

5. See William Hubben, Dostoevsky, Kierkegaard, Nietzsche, and Kafka. New York: Collier Books, 1962, p. 40. First published in 1952.

6. Verker i utvalg, III, p. 164.

7. Ibid., p. 168.

8. See Jean-Paul Sartre, L'Etre et le néant. Paris: Gallimard, 1943, pp. 449–50.

9. Verker i utvalg, III, p. 168.

10. Ibid., p. 174.

11. Verker i utvalg, II, p. 13.

12. Verker i utvalg, III, p. 181. My italics.

13. Sartre, L'Etre et le néant, p. 464.

14. Verker i utvalg, III, p. 182.

15. Ibid., p. 196.

16. Ibid., p. 280.

17. Ibid., p. 186.

18. Ibid., p. 315.

19. Ibid., p. 325.

20. Ibid., p. 184.

21. Ibid., p. 188.

22. Ibid., p. 197.

23. Ibid., p. 202.

24. Ibid., p. 191.

25. Ibid., p. 202. My italics.

26. Ibid., p. 203.

27. Ibid., p. 217.

28. Ibid., p. 208.

29. Ibid., p. 209.

30. Ibid., p. 214. Sandemose's italics.

31. Ibid., p. 210.

32. Ibid., p. 243.

33. Ibid., p. 257.

34. Ibid., p. 320.

35. Ibid., p. 332.

36. Ibid.

37. Ibid., p. 333.

4.

A Fugitive Crosses His Tracks:
Confrontation with Jante

With A Fugitive Crosses His Tracks Sandemose experienced both an artistic and psychological breakthrough. The novel was a critical and commercial success; and Sandemose wrote it in the first-person singular, for the first time concentrating upon the central themes of childhood and adolescence. In his previous works Sandemose dealt sparingly and reluctantly with the past. For example, in A Sailor Goes Ashore Espen never ventured beyond the murder of John Wakefield in Misery Harbor and the beatings on the deck of the "Rurik." In A Fugitive, however, the narrator overcomes his reticence to admit what is really troubling him, and his very first line of the novel, "Now I shall tell all,"[1] illustrates his desire to withhold nothing and spare no one, however painful the process. A Fugitive is a wrenchingly personal investigation of problems which were of utmost significance to Sandemose, namely the genesis of the individual during childhood and adolescence. The book is a blistering attack on early twentieth-century society--home, school, and other centers of authority which, according to the narrator, cripple the individual's potential for natural growth and joyful expansion. A Freudian consideration of childhood as the source of adult neurosis goes hand in hand with a penetrating social observation of the laws and patterns according to which modern society functions.

The novel was first published in 1933. A revised version appeared as volume two of Verker i utvalg in 1955. During the two decades separating the editions, some of Sandemose's bitterness had subsided. As a result his vision became more objective. In the 1955 edition observation and commentary are emphasized, whereas the original version focuses on psychological destruction during

childhood and adolescence. The respective subtitles confirm this
shift. In 1933 Sandemose preferred "the story of a murderer's
childhood." In 1955 he changed this subtitle to "Espen Arnakke's
commentaries upon the Jante Law." Nevertheless, essentially the
novel has remained the same.[2] In both versions Sandemose describes
Espen Arnakke's childhood and youth in the small Danish town,
Jante, his subsequent years as a sailor, and his ultimate
confrontation with John Wakefield at Misery Harbor. In both
versions Espen attempts to put his past in order so as to
understand what turned him into a murderer. In both versions Espen
the narrator succeeds in liberating himself sufficiently from the
past so as to construct a radically different future. Neither
version describes in detail what this new future would entail. As
the basic text I shall use the 1933 edition, occasionally referring
to the later one to clarify a point.

The Search for Objectivity

In A Fugitive the narrator intervenes frequently, measuring
the temporal and psychological distance between his present and
past selves, professing faith in the future while desiring to reach
a point where he can let the past sink into oblivion. This clearly
will only be possible once the story has been told completely and
with scrupulous honesty. The narrator refers to himself as an
"illusionist," "scorpion," and "worm."[3] He desperately wishes to
tell the truth, but does he? Is he not rather distorting the past
in a subconscious attempt to cover feelings of inadequacy and
guilt? "There was a story that I for a long time loved to tell
about a friend of mine who committed murder because he was mistreated as a small boy. It was fiction."[4] Is he using his poison-
ous stinger to take revenge on a society which had failed to love
and appreciate him? Or is he in fact resuscitating the demons of
the past because they provide him with a rich source of inspiration
as a narrator? "But I often wonder whether it really was so bad in
those days, for when there is nobody else to scream at, one screams
at his demons and becomes their bosom friend--."[5] The 1955 edition
is clearer and stronger: ". . . for when there is nobody else to
scream at, you scream at your demons and conjure them up, you use
them, you conjure them up and take as your servants precisely those
demons who are out to ruin you."[6] The narrator's goal is to rid
himself of his ulterior motives, to extinguish his own ego in order
to prevent it from distorting the story and make it subjective, to
suppress his desire to sting and wound. He wishes to be nothing
but a worm possessing a human voice:

"Inside my brain a worm is crawling, it is three centimeters
long and about as thick as my little finger. It is boring its way
through and is always in slow motion, its head is the soft and pale
head of a child, and it always keeps its eyes closed as if it were
sleeping. It lives from my memories from the time when I first
signed on a ship until I fled from Misery Harbor. Each time it
comes upon such a memory, it lies down comfortably to eat.

Gradually it has chewed them all and digested them several times. I wish I could take the worm and let it speak about its meals, it would be a strange tale, and just imagine a small voice like that speaking the truth, the first truth in the world. I wanted to record the words so that they could never be distorted by believers and nonbelievers."[7]

Even at the end of the novel, however, Sandemose's narrator must recognize that he is far from his goal. Instead of being that of a worm having digested Espen's childhood memories, his point of view is that of a slave chained to the ground, limited and subjective, conditioned by his continuing misery. The narrative, then, has not completely liberated the story teller. His situation remains that of a chained slave attempting to comprehend the meaning of the mountain he observes before him in an effort to understand what he is seeing: "I have been around it on a hunting trip, and it is curious to see how such a mountain has become completely different from what it used to be each time one has moved a bit and looks at it again. You may get a thousand different descriptions of Halfway Mountain and they are all equally correct. I feel a strong urge to tell you this now, that the mountain is big and has many sides, but the one who lay chained on the ground saw Halfway Mountain only from the side where he was lying."[8] Halfway Mountain is, of course, life itself, which the narrator feels unable to observe in all its richness because of his limited, unprivileged perspective.

The past does not return to the narrator as a coherent chronological whole, but rather as a series of uncoordinated images. Sandemose compares the resulting novel to an archeological site where only fragments have been uncovered, and where most of the old structures have been irretrievably lost. The author of the 1955 edition realizes that even the fragments which have been uncovered are, to a certain extent, reconstructed by the narrator/archeologist, and that no account of the past can possibly escape the influence of the present: "Even when I had written the book for the first time it appeared to me as a piece of archeology, something it was to become later in a completely different way as well, since new layers were formed on top of the completed work."[9] According to the preface Sandemose wrote for the 1955 edition, the truth is "written in water": "Everything makes its marks, large and small ones, and life itself may appear to be a mirage, everything gets displaced, nothing remains the same from one hour to the next. The world changes in the wink of an eye."[10]

To Sandemose, life is change, and any attempt to present it as fixed within a formal mold results in distortion.[11] Consistent with this view, Sandemose was ever eager to redo his works, presenting fragments from different points of view, uncovering additional ones, and relegating others, which he had formerly considered to be of great significance, to humbler places. Sandemose consistently refused to call A Fugitive Crosses His Tracks a novel, since, to him, a novel is a molded image of life. He rejected this formal perfection, because he wished his art to be a faithful reflection of the formlessness and contingent nature of life itself.

In A Fugitive formalism is Sandemose's chief target. Jante, Sandemose's symbol of modern industrialized society, functions according to a rigid, unwritten law, which cripples the individual's potential for natural growth and transforms him or her into a cog. The focus of the book is on the working classes, who, in Sandemose's view, have lost the self-esteem which would lead them to active rebellion. All of Jante functions according to an absurd, inhuman rhythm, symbolized by the shrieking sound of the factory siren at precisely the same hour every morning and the unchangeable patter of the workers' march through the streets of the town: "I always was amazed at the great precision of all the workers. The one who arrived five minutes early did so all his life, every day, five minutes early. And the one who arrived one minute early never changed either, he arrived one minute early every day for forty years. The poor fellow whose fate it was to arrive half a minute too late was in the same boat in his own way, he came running with his tongue hanging out of his mouth, half a minute late every day during a couple of generations. It had to be like that. The world order could not be changed."[12] Particularly frightening is that the working people of Jante have permitted the terror to affect them so profoundly that they have ceased to question its cause and have become collaborators in their own destruction.

Jante

Sandemose compares the Jante law to the law of Moses. Both derive from an intangible authority, both are repetitious and generally prohibitory. Both strike the monotonous refrain, "You shall not . . . ." The Jante law pitches you against we. Its terrifying power derives from the fact that every inhabitant of Jante must confront the hostile, anonymous, judging group.[13]

While reflecting upon the murder of John Wakefield in Misery Harbor, the narrator realizes that a connection exists between the murder and his upbringing in Jante. In fact, the murder of John Wakefield was Espen's ultimate act of revolt against the Jante law. Once the act was done, Espen must "cross his tracks," return to the source of the problem, and attempt to understand how he became the person he is. What reasons lie behind his symbolic landing in Misery Harbor?

While in the preface to the 1955 edition Sandemose admits that Jante is modeled on "the town Nykøbing on the island of Mors,"[14] he nevertheless insists that Jante is no particular town, because it can be any town: "But Jante was everywhere, it was on the prairie in Canada, it spread across the U.S.A., it bloomed in Jevnaker and flourished in Jutland. One surely didn't avoid it by fleeing."[15]

Characteristically, Jante is a colorless and grey place, where every inhabitant lives a hellish existence in perpetual fear of everyone else. The mentality is to maintain power over others to prevent them from overpowering you.[16] All positive values are denied: "The effort to seal ignorance is called the road towards the heights and the eternal longing."[17] The 1955 edition is more specific: "Knowledge was something despicable. Art was judged with a sneer. Science was something that occupied the lazy."[18] Work is a chore, something to avoid at any cost: "Never hurry, that was the refrain all day long, every day, all days . . . ."[19] The Jante mentality creates a complete lack of self-confidence, a resentment against work, a hatred of more privileged groups, and a thirst for revenge; it undermines the child's moral fiber and stimulates its violent tendencies. The spectrum of society described in A Fugitive is profoundly disturbing. In order to underscore the spiritual crippling of the place, the narrator frequently portrays people who are physically repulsive. The detestable aunt Oline, for instance, is described in the following way: "Oline was always red in the head from one insult or another, she has a spot on her chin, she tossed her head and wrinkled her lips."[20] Oline is physically stained, and her infernal personality colors the skin of her head red. Oline is Espen's childhood demon, constantly torturing him.

    Having lost their soul, the inhabitants of Jante resemble animals, meat, or lifeless objects. For example, Espen's friend, Latterfrosken (Laughing Frog): "He resembled a frog, his eyes perched like two plums, almost no forehead."[21] The arch-hypocrite, Skyldfri (Guiltless) Sidenius cries in the following way: "Skyldfri made her several hundred kilograms vibrate, let out a tentative howl like a dog and continued by making rattling, lapping noises like those of an harpooned whale."[22] A watchman and his wife symbolize the rigidity of the townspeople: "The wife was stalking along, greyish white and square, with enormous amounts of clothes on, and her hymn book in her handkerchief. She was very straight and rectangular. Her face was fixed in an imbecile sneer, the watchman saw nothing but the ground in front of him."[23] Sandemose emphasizes the artificial movements, the grey, rigid forms, and the limited vision of the couple, true citizens of Jante. The most grotesque description is nevertheless that of Paul Himmelby, an alcoholic whose human potential has been totally destroyed, reducing the man to "a gigantic, swampy sack who was drooling on himself and had a head like a rotten watermelon."[24] In the 1955 edition the description of Paul Himmelby is even more repulsive, an indication that Sandemose's hatred of Jante has in no way diminished.

    How do people in Jante manage to survive it all? The answer is simple: most are not even aware of their condition. They exist on envy and cover up imagined inferiority through bluff: "The Jante man cannot get up. Instead he is bluffing. He bluffs others into believing that he is as big as he really is. He himself does not believe it."[25] This tactic, unfortunately, signifies not

victory over Jante but submission to it. Only an occasional misfit
appears to be impervious to the environment. "Jenny the Terrorist"
retains her individuality, while the half German, Vilfred, escapes
because, by heredity, he is an outsider: "Fresh and unembarrassed
Vilfred was always moving ahead towards his goal, without beating
around the bush, while we were squirming like worms. His questions
to the adults were direct, he looked them straight in the eye,
until he received an answer.

     "We didn't like it. He was a stranger."[26] In his favorite
movie Espen observes a jocular boy who refuses to conform to the
rules of adults. Secretly the laughing boy becomes Espen's hero,
though he himself is far too intimidated to follow the boy's
example in life. In the 1955 edition, the narrator expresses overt
sympathy and even a feeling of identity with those who escape
Jante. For instance there is Tjue-Frans (Frans the Thief), one day
observed by Espen saving three children from drowning. Tjue-Frans
simply does not understand the structure of Jante and the behavior
that is expected of him. He fails to see that his generous act
will be interpreted as an attempt to "show off," to prove that he
is better than those who have chosen to observe the event
detachedly from the sidelines. Because of his unwillingness to
learn the rules of the game, Tjue-Frans becomes immune to the
poison of Jante: "He could stand in front of people, as if out of
reach, all you did passed him by, be it angry words or friendliness. Tjue-Frans paid no attention to it, he bowed and said thank
you whatever they hit upon, he was thinking of something else, and
then they became very angry."[27] For Espen, Tjue-Frans is a hero,
gracious as a gazelle and with lively eyes. He is anti-Jante,
possessing the kind of freedom that Espen longs after: "Tjue-Frans
has meant so endlessly much to me, he became a warning against
rapid judgments, and a moral beacon."[28]

     Unfortunately, Espen is far different from Jenny, Vilfred, the
laughing boy, and Frans. He responds to Jante exactly the way he
is supposed to, becomes an easy victim of the terror, and suffers
repeated humiliation and defeat. In fact, he wishes to adapt and
conform, and when he finally leaves Jante in desperation, he does
so in hopes of returning one day as a respected citizen. His
notion of triumph over the town is by returning a success, not
realizing for a minute that this sort of triumph is in reality submission.

     Fleeing Jante, Espen is seized by a sense of loss: "For the
boy who was standing on the ship looking towards the disappearing
land realized that all hopes and visions, all wishes of life and
death, had been tied with an umbilical cord to the places which belonged to his childhood. Now he was away from those places and was
a broken man."[29] Like Thor and the Klabautermann, Espen feels that
he has been expelled from his home: "My eyes were clinging to the
disappearing land, the hills billowing over a grey sky, all my
dreams were shot down like birds in the raw, ice cold morning, down
into an icy world which was never to see summer again."[30] Arriving

in a foreign city he feels miserable: "These houses and these streets are cold and foreign. I am expelled, placed outside of life."[31] Away from Jante, Espen feels exiled from life, and his most ardent desire is to return and settle down. It is the murder of John Wakefield in Misery Harbor and the subsequent self-analysis he goes through, which will make him realize that the future must be made for him far from the town. The self-analysis, the composition of the story, will of course return him home, but in the process fascination with Jante will peel away, and he finally is able to look for more fertile ground in which to plant his roots.

Fairyland

Sandemose structures his novels upon the myth of expulsion from Eden, to which the exile longs to return. With Jante the loss and longing are parodied. The town orchards contain the apples that Espen and his friends are perpetually coveting. In fact, stealing apples is the favorite pastime of the adolescent boys of Jante. The narrator refers to the lost Eden as Fairyland, and he associates it with warm sunshine and the good smell of tar from a fisherman's net: "The barred rocks by the elderberry bushes were the heart of Fairyland. Warmth exuded from the place and the sun was always shining there."[32] The narrator recalls the Eve of Fairyland, a four-year old child called Rose, whose chief attribute is her beauty. Rose's family is pious, and her most important concern is whether she merits heaven. Espen's stay in Fairyland is brief indeed. It ends abruptly when, as a small boy himself, he discovers Rose playing with a group of girls. Tormented by jealousy Espen is seized by an uncontrollable desire to shock Rose, and he utters a swear word to her: "'Hell,' I said suddenly and looked stiffly at Rose. For I knew that her mother didn't like anybody to swear."[33] Rose's reaction is immediate and final: "'Yes, you are mean,' said Rose seriously. It sounded as if it was something she had always known. 'I don't want to play with you. You will not go to God.'"[34] Espen in turn has a keen experience of falling from a state of grace: "At once I felt stupid and ugly, and had never heard it before. I left with downturned eyes."[35] The narrator explains Espen's fall in terms of a changed self-image. Without resistance he believes Rose's words. He feels ugly, abnormal, and stupid, and everyone confirms the accuracy of his fallen image. Rose/Eve symbolizes the conformity of Jante. In Sandemose's version of the Eden myth, Rose/Eve is no temptress. She smugly sides with God and remains in the garden, while Espen/Adam is declared an undesirable person and expelled. In order to return to the state of grace, Espen must rid himself of his degraded self-image; he must again be able to see himself as a normal, healthy, intelligent individual.

Espen's break with Rose symbolically lands him in Misery Harbor for the first time. Driven by what Poe refers to as the "imp of the perverse," the child Espen swears in front of Rose, knowing full well what her reaction will be. Even in Fairyland,

Espen is victim of his jealousy, of a desire to possess exclusively another human being; on her side Rose is possessed by conventional fear of breaking the ten commandments and therefore being excluded from heaven. At the age of four, both Espen and Rose are already victims of Jante, conditioned by dogmas and laws that hinder the natural growth and expansion of the personality. Moreover, while Rose never questions her Sunday school proscriptions, Espen is already a rebel, defying convention and knowing full well that his defiance will result in expulsion from Fairyland and bring him endless misery.

The Fairyland of Espen and Rose was not an authentic Eden, for its inhabitants were not innocent. The authentic Fairyland nevertheless continues to exist as a dream in the narrator's heart: "Fairyland, Genesis, is merely a dream in his heart, a blind dream carved in amber and in gold."[36] Is this image a lost paradise, or does it exist solely in the mind? In the course of the novel Espen does have brief periods during which he feels in touch with a life form completely different from that of diurnal Jante. Espen has an extraordinary sensitivity to nature, from the sound of the wind in the trees to the smell of the soil. The paradise which Espen senses is close to nature, consequently far removed from the strictures of Jante. It is associated with an expansive, positive attitude towards life, in stark contrast to the life-denying Jante spirit. In fact, it is these fragmentary experiences of Fairyland that save Espen from being absorbed in the quagmire of Jante: "You shall remember that you have been a child. You shall remember Fairyland, that you have to establish a defense and get through alive."[37] To uncover the sham in order to reach down to the hard and naked reality is the purpose of the narrator's long fragmented account. His aim is to dig deep enough to reach solid ground upon which he will be able to start constructing the house of the future, the only Fairyland which has lasting value to him.

Father and Son

In any examination of disturbed childhood the home naturally plays a major role. Espen's father is a decent, conscientious worker, struggling to make ends meet for his large family. The narrator's image of the father is fairly complex, influenced by Sandemose's interest in Freud. On the one hand, the father serves as a model for the son, an individual who has succeeded in surviving Jante without losing his humanity: "Still, I can see my father there in the street, a cog in the machine, but with his own life. He had preserved it. The factory had not had the power to kill his soul. He was the best and wisest man I met in Fairyland, with a mildness so great that he still is my model in my best moments."[38] The father's decision to accept his place within the social group represents in fact a rebellion against <u>his</u> own father, a dreamer and artist who felt so mistreated by society that he rejected it altogether. Sandemose then places Espen within a chain of father-son relationships. In each generation the son is fated to rebel against his father. Since Espen's father has suppressed the rebellious tendencies within himself and assumed the role of the solid citizen, Espen must become a social outcast, a dreamer-artist like his grandfather.

In Espen's mind, the father represents a great force, a powerful Khan or almighty God. The narrator recalls a dream of Espen's from early childhood: "A few of us boys were standing on the road when a terrible horse appeared. It had an enormous head, and long, sharp teeth hanging down like a beard. All the other boys got away from it, but it squeezed me into a corner and said to me: I shall eat you if you don't always go to bed at ten o'clock."[39] The horse who is attempting to make the child submit to his authority is the father. Elsewhere in the novel, Espen witnesses a stallion who is hit by lightning and has its leg torn off. Again the horse is associated with the father. The horrible sight inspires ambivalent feelings in the child--on the one hand, pity for the crippled animal, on the other hand, the sensation of fulfillment: "this is as well the rebellious wish of the child, the child who wanted to sit mightily in the sky and strike with lightning all the big and strong ones."[40] The child here associates himself with the outcast Thor taking revenge on his oppressors by flailing his hammer in the sky.

The association between the father and the horse is clearly sexual. This becomes even more obvious if we compare the description of the legless horse to an incident which takes place in A Sailor Goes Ashore, where Old Bodilsen's huge stallion assaults and kills Sten Eriksen's tiny mare. In a last, desperate attempt to defend herself, the mare bites into the stallion's sex organ, thereby destroying the powerful animal forever. Interestingly enough, the castrated stallion belongs to Gjatrid's father, and the maiming of the horse represents, as in A Fugitive, the desire to revolt against a powerful father figure. The mythic incarnation of the horse-man are the Greek centaurs, often represented in art as "drawing the chariot of the wine god Dionysus or bound and ridden by Eros, the god of love, in allusion to their drunken and amorous habits."[41]

Espen frequently refers to his father's sexuality, the most obvious proof being the nine children he has sired. Nevertheless, the parents themselves have instilled in the child the notion that sexuality is evil, and Espen is torn between the desire to taste the fruit and a parental-inspired vision of purity. His ambivalent attitude towards his father profoundly affects his emotions towards his mother. While wishing his mother to be pure, he at the same time nourishes oedipal feelings towards her: "Mother has given birth to us, but father had no part of it. One wanted to be closest to his mother, nobody else must be closer. One elevates himself to be the father, but of course he exists, and one climbs another step, making oneself into God the father--and becomes one's own father."[42] In order to explain his point more clearly, the narrator refers to the story of the birth of Jesus, and the dogma of the Trinity, according to which the mystical Christ was his own father.

Espen's preoccupations with parental sexuality are rooted in profound frustration. Sex is the forbidden fruit of a frightening, secret garden approached at the risk of eternal damnation. During the pre-puberty years, masturbation provides Espen with an outlet for his frustration. The experience, however, inevitably ends in disappointment, followed by shame and fear of terrible punishment.

The masturbation phase comes abruptly to an end the day Espen is confirmed, not because he has outgrown the practice but because confirmation in Jante heralds the time for conquering members of the other sex. Sandemose views confirmation as a primitive initiation ritual, a ceremony which is supposed to transform the boy into a grown man. Since sexuality was a forbidden topic in the home, Espen had to glean his knowledge from a peer group as misinformed as himself. All girls automatically become objects that the boys are supposed to seduce in the woods in order to have something to boast about on streetcorners the following day. All of Espen's sexual adventures are failures; and in order to face himself and his friends he finds consolation in long, lonely nights in the woods consuming huge amounts of alcohol, another outlet his father has strictly forbidden.

Adamsen's Barn

In A Fugitive Espen's sexuality is clearly linked to the recurring motif of Adamsen's barn. Adamsen's barn is further associated with Abraham's field in A Sailor Goes Ashore, the place where Espen and Kristine experienced their all-consuming erotic encounter. Furthermore, it was in the barn that Sten made love to Maja, thereby sealing his right of ownership. Adamsen's barn is veiled in mystery. It is associated with God and Lucifer, love and hatred, fire and destruction. A stone in its exterior wall becomes in Espen's mind "the holy stone," providing, so he believes, an entrance into Fairyland. While the narrator never reveals completely the mystery surrounding Adamsen's barn, he associates the place with transgression against Espen's father, who did not want the children to play there. The memory of the barn also evokes that of Espen's younger sister, Agnes: "In Adamsen's barn Agnes and I had a cave in the hay. It was good to taste the forbidden fruit in the forbidden house. There was a weak light in our cave, we had made a little screen, a Persian blind, so that we could look down on the barn floor and know what was going on there and who was in the barn. Around us mice were puttering around. On the beams the ermine was walking and was the strange spirit of the house.

"It was the great bliss."[43] The imagery suggests incest. Espen and Agnes eat the forbidden fruit in the place where the father had specifically told them not to enter. Moreover, the narrator refers to Adamsen's barn as the House of the Father.[44] The

Biblical story of Adam and Eve is of course a story of incest as well, since the archetypal couple were siblings. In Sandemose's version Adam is the father, and he is claiming possession of Eve/Agnes, his daughter. The transgressor is Cain, the son, who wishes to take Eve/Agnes away from his father. Though veiled, the incestuous imagery is fairly obvious; it is a desire that the narrator never manages to face. Instead he opts for destroying the barn through purifying fire: "I stand looking into the semi-obscure barn. Crawling like worms we got in there . . . into my father's barn. Yes, I am moving at the edge of something I do not know. My father didn't have a barn. I have become someone else. The fugitive has returned and will cross his tracks, but he cannot go through the fire in Adamsen's barn."[45]

An interesting contrast to the barn motif in A Fugitive is an episode which takes place in Newfoundland after Espen has killed John Wakefield. Fleeing the place of the murder, Espen hits upon a house where a fisherman, Walter Shece, lives with his daughter Ishbel. Ishbel in fact offers herself to Espen. Welcoming the young man into his house, the father does not object to Espen's relationship to his daughter, and encourages a marriage between the two. Walter Shece and Ishbel offer Espen a taste of sexuality without transgression, but subsequently, and with no explanation, Shece withdraws the offer. Espen runs away from the house; yet the narrator looks back upon the experience with nostalgia: "But now I know that at Walter Shece's I had for a short while entered Adamsen's barn, it was warm and snug and did not burn."[46]

In spite of his short adventure with Ishbel, eroticism remains for Espen a symbol of all that was wrong with his upbringing in Jante. It represents power, the need to impose one's authority on another. It is the glorification of the strong and thrives on con-frontation. It is in this sense that the narrator's comment in the 1955 edition must be interpreted: "When I said that the Jante religion was a worship of Phallus, I meant that it was behind most of it."[47] It is significant that one of Espen's last acts before leaving Jante was to drag a heavy, ugly bench on which he had failed so miserably to perform his acts of seduction, down to the pier and dump it into the sea: "What a splash! . . . I stormed into the woods and drew a breath of relief. I was tripping hap-pily."[48] The act is symbolic, a physical protest against Jante. It underscores once again Espen's frustration and need to rebel; it foreshadows the attack on John Wakefield in Misery Harbor. By killing John, Espen confronts Jante head on; as a result he becomes a criminal, a haunted man. However, as Louis Kronenberger points out in his review of The Fugitive in The New York Times, Espen "was too early imbued with a sense of guilt, to be turned overnight into a haunted man. He was one already. Long before he could have felt that the world had a warrant out for him as a murderer, he felt it had one out for him as Espen Arnakke." Sandemose chose this statement as an epigraph for the 1955 edition of the novel. Since childhood Espen has been made to feel that he was an outcast.

By becoming one in fact he lives up to the expectations others appeared to have had for him.[49]

Pathetically enough, Espen's parents were themselves instrumental in instilling the unfortunate self-image in their son. Espen's father tells him about a childhood incident, where the boy's mother had dreamed that a townsman, the evil Jens Nordhammer, had won the baby in a confrontation with Death: "He pointed out that death and the evil element in the world had been fighting for me--and I stayed alive."[50] The father's words mark Espen profoundly, making him believe that he is indeed possessed by evil, and that he would have been better off had he been permitted to die as an infant.

The significance of the Nordhammer incident is great, since it symbolizes the guilt of Espen's parents in failing to protect their young son from evil in the world. They are themselves victims of superstitious beliefs, and help instill in their son a dangerous, negative self-image. The evil element to which the parents abandon their son is Jante, for Espen's parents are too weak to protect him against the Jante forces. The struggle takes place within the home itself, where the weaker and smaller children become the victims of the older and stronger ones: "I know what it was that made the old ones relinquish their power. They themselves did not believe that they were doing it. They didn't want to 'meddle,' which means that one supports the stronger party. They wanted to be <u>neutral</u>, and thought that such a thing existed. They knew nothing about the nature of neutrality. They were fighting for peace in the home, and handed over the weak ones to Moloch. They wanted peace, but behind this was hidden their fear of Oline, which was as strong as our fear, and, among frightened people you can expect no solidarity."[51]

<u>A Fugitive</u> marks for Sandemose the end of a long road backwards. He is addressing a socio-psychological problem--the destruction of the individual personality by the social conformism of small town life--that he shares with millions of others. The aim of the book is to undermine structures which stifle positive human expansion. As a narrator, Espen takes obvious pleasure in swinging his thunderbolt hard and heavy. His writing has become a hammer that will wreak revenge upon the Jantes of the world. Interestingly enough, the narrator strikes his main blows at the working class itself. What distresses him is the breakdown of the victims' moral fiber, a breakdown which has turned the powerless against each other instead of uniting them against their common oppressors within modern society.

Notes

1. Aksel Sandemose, En flyktning krysser sitt spor. Fortelling om en morders barndom. Oslo: Tiden Norsk Forlag, 1933, p. 5.

2. I disagree with Yngvar Ustvedt's statement in his preface to his 1967 edition of the original version of the novel, that the 1955 edition is in fact a totally different work. See Aksel Sandemose, En flyktning krysser sitt spor. Oslo: H. Aschehoug and Co., 1967, p. XV.

3. En flyktning krysser sitt spor, pp. 119, 257, 420.

4. Ibid., p. 420.

5. Ibid., p. 442.

6. 1955 edition. Verker i utvalg, II, p. 479. Sandemose's italics.

7. En flyktning krysser sitt spor, p. 420.

8. Ibid., p. 452.

9. 1955 edition. Verker i utvalg, II, p. 14.

10. Ibid., p. 17.

11. This view is similar to that of Proust and the "new novelists" in France.

12. En flyktning krysser sitt spor, p. 33.

13. The conflict between the individual and the group is one of the major themes in modern fiction.

14. 1955 edition. Verker i utvalg, II, p. 12.

15. En flyktning krysser sitt spor, p. 96. See also 1955 edition. Verker i utvalg, II, p. 13.

16. This type of powerplay is frequently encountered in the work of Sartre. See for example L'Etre et le néant, pp. 462-63.

17. En flyktning krysser sitt spor, p. 152.

18. 1955 edition. Verker i utvalg, II, p. 135.

19. Ibid., p. 261.

20. En flyktning krysser sitt spor, p. 91.

21. Ibid., p. 206.

22. Ibid., p. 356.

23. Ibid., p. 106.

24. Ibid., p. 44.

25. 1955 edition. Verker i utvalg, II, p. 82.

26. Ibid., p. 362.

27. Ibid., pp. 258-59.

28. Ibid., p. 258.

29. En flyktning krysser sitt spor, p. 405.

30. Ibid.

31. Ibid., pp. 405-06.

32. Ibid., p. 8.

33. Ibid., p. 7.

34. Ibid.

35. Ibid.

36. Ibid., p. 230.

37. Ibid., p. 288. Sandemose's italics.

38. Ibid., p. 14.

39. Ibid., p. 319. For a detailed interpretation of the associations between the father and the horse, see Høyt på en vinget hest, pp. 95-100.

40. En flyktning krysser sitt spor, p. 320.

41. Encyclopaedia Brittanica. 15th edition. Chicago: Encyclopaedia Brittanica, Inc., p. 679.

42. En flyktning krysser sitt spor, p. 216.

43. Ibid., p. 194.

44. Ibid., p. 197.

45. Ibid., p. 193.

46. Ibid., p. 280.

47. 1955 edition. Verker i utvalg, II, p. 208.

48. Ibid., p. 352.

49. Jean-Paul Sartre, Saint-Genêt, translated by Bernard
Frechtman. New York: Braziller, 1963, pp. 71-85.

50. En flyktning krysser sitt spor, p. 412.

51. Ibid., p. 95.

5.

Horns for Our Adornment:
The Taming of the Beast

According to Sandemose, <u>Horns for Our Adornment</u> represents <u>The Klabautermann</u> in its final form. Once more the setting is a sailing ship, this time known as "Fulton." Brief poetic texts, sometimes enriching the main story, sometimes digressive, interpose themselves upon the narrative. Thus the story line is fragmented and symbolic. The author paints a stark picture of life on board the ship that carries cargo back and forth from Iceland. Representing widely different personality types and social backgrounds, the six-man crew must cope collectively with storms, disasters, and death, not to mention a steadily increasing sexual frustration and tense interpersonal situations. Pascal's famous statement, "Nous sommes tous embarqués,"[1] of our all sharing the same boat--readily comes to mind. The tension reaches its peak when, during a stay in Eskefjord in Iceland, each of the crew members falls in love with a single girl, "Helga the fair." With her heavy blonde braid, silver hair ornament, and horse, Helga incarnates a dream; she is lifted directly from <u>Gunnlaugs saga ormstungu</u>, where Gunnlaugr and Hrafn are fighting for her, only to lose her to a third man. "Helga was blonde. The skipper became poetic and thought she fit so well in between these grey mountains and light nights."[2] In the sailors' fantasies, Helga remains a mystery, a "Holy Virgin," whose purity they venture to transgress symbolically and in thoughts and dreams. Frustration produces such physical tension that the "Fulton"'s captain, the wealthy and refined Claes Winckel, becomes seriously ill and must spend several weeks in the Eskefjord hospital. Ultimately the ship leaves Eskefjord without Helga, and continues its restless journey across the ocean. The crew breaks apart when each of the sailors decides to leave the ship and go his own way. Resenting what he considers to be a personal betrayal, the normally restrained Winckel turns violent and pushes one of the deck hands,

the giant Gullhesten (Goldhorse), overboard to his death. The
novel concludes poetically with Gullhesten's death vision, followed
by a second vision in which the narrator points out a possible
direction for the future.

Exposure to Death

In addition to Captain Winckel and Gullhesten, the crew consists of Karsten Dal, the young mate fresh from officer's school,
the cook, a person of Finnish stock (a kven), and two additional
deck hands, Bjarne Vik, a North Norwegian, and Johannes Hansen,
alias the Pastor, who was ejected from his parish in Norway after a
rape attempt upon a young girl. As in The Klabautermann, the ship
is an image of the world; it is the sailor's only protection
against the seemingly endless ocean that is ever threatening to
swallow him up: "The ship is the world. It is so small that we
feel it pulling us along."[3] Each of the sailors is an outsider who
has failed to integrate into conventional society and construct
around himself the illusion of safety provided by home and family.
On the ship the crew is constantly exposed to the violence of
nature and human frailty. Death never is far away. One of the
central episodes in the novel describes the young mate's fatal fall
from the mast onto the deck of the ship. While the sailors fear
death, they also are fascinated by it. The narrator romanticizes
the sailor as an explorer, perpetually searching for the ineffable
in life: "He is searching for something whose innermost core is
peace, he chases it madly."[4] Total peace can be only death, and at
times the crew is tempted to end the voyage by permitting the ship
to dissolve into the ocean. Seated high on the mast one day, the
Pastor experiences the following thoughts: "If I fall now, I'll
disappear at once. Just as surely as if I fell into melted lead.
The sea will return nothing. A few flops, and then finished,
knocked down by the waves, a last uneasy feeling, a few foolish
looking flops, until I am down where it is very still."[5] After
Karsten Dal's death, Claes Winckel wishes to spend a stormy night
alone on the deck: "But the skipper wanted to be alone in the dark
realm of death, he was standing on the rail his arms entwined in
the sideboards, looking at the ocean. He stood like that for
several hours. Then he went over to the galley and stood there.
He was looking at the wild ocean, and didn't have a thought."[6]
When at the end of the novel Gullhesten falls from the deck into
the small boat waiting to take him to shore, his head splits open
and he screams with happiness: "He never woke up again. He tumbled down into the darkness, but the fall was loaded with light.
The light focused on an image of himself. He screamed with happiness."[7]

More frequently, however, the constant threat of death causes
the crew to huddle together in the small cabin, seeking protection
from fear in each other's company. During the night following the
mate's funeral, all except the captain smoke and play cards: "Here

the living were sitting together protected against the dead ones
who were calling in the storm.

"Little was said. They were smoking and said only the most
essential things about the cards. The Pastor was permitted to
join, and was spared a dressing down when he made a fool of himself.

"Death tied the living together."[8]

The Crew

A ship's crew customarily lacks social permanence, and a
sailor will tend to wander from crew to crew in search of elusive
peace. Exceptional in this respect, the crew in The Klabautermann
stayed together from year to year; as long as Anna was on the ship
none of the crew members wanted to leave. According to Gullhesten
in Horns for Our Adornment, a woman and children provide the only
stabilizing element in the existence of the restless male. The
lack of family support was what drove Espen Arnakke away from
Jante, and he only found peace by marrying Gjatrid and founding a
family of his own. The family relieves the problem of anguish and
loneliness and offers the wanderer a measure of peace. A ship's
crew can at times serve as surrogate family, but its impermanence
is caused by lack of the essential unifying element, wife and
mother.

The Rat

In many ways the crew of the "Fulton" is different from other
groups described by Sandemose. None of the six men on board has
been cursed with the name Thor, its derivations, or other associations with the Norse god. While the crew members are outsiders in
varying degrees, they are not genuine outcasts comparable to Adam
Klinte in The Klabautermann. While the Pastor comes closest to
this definition, there are efforts made to integrate him into the
group rather than throw him out. In fact, the archetypal scapegoat
in Horns for Our Adornment is not a human being at all, but a rat
which has somehow managed to enter the ship: "Above them was the
arch of a clear and still wintry sky. On all sides the deserted
ocean across a hundred miles. In the middle lay the 'Fulton,' a
small world in infinite space. The last five persons in the world
were fanatically chasing a rat."[10] The rat incarnates the
Klabautermann, desperately attempting to make himself a home on the
ship. The rat displays amazing ingenuity in its attempts to avoid
its persecutors. It laughs at their traps, bites two of the
sailors, and manages miraculously to disappear each time one of the
crew members believes he has caught it. Ultimately, however, the
hunt wears down the rodent and it starts searching for another
ship: "It looks around nervously for more inviting ships."[11] In
the end, one of the sailors catches the rat and throws it into the

sea. The rat makes a final effort to swim towards the "Fulton," but the distance steadily increases until it completely disappears from view. The ideal social group would, according to Sandemose, be humane enough to welcome the rat into its midst. However, the world must first cease being viewed in terms of hunter and hunted. The distinction between strong and weak must be wiped out. If the strong would no longer exercise authority over the weak, the weak would abandon its determination to take revenge. A rat would no longer have to behave like a rat.[12] The result would, of course, be the end of Jante, to be replaced by a truly humane society.

The Captain

At first glance the most civilized person on the "Fulton" appears to be its captain. There seems to be little similarity between the refined, handsome Claes Winckel and the rough, homely Adam Klinte in The Klabautermann: "Nature has lavished its gifts upon Claes Winckel and created the almost perfect human being . . . ."[13] More than any other Sandemose character to this point, Winckel bears similarity to Sten Eriksen in A Sailor Goes Ashore. Both are representatives of the educated upper bourgeoisie, and their privileged backgrounds have instilled in them a tolerance and self-assurance unheard of in the deprived working classes from which most of Sandemose's characters derive. All through Sandemose's work, there is a certain hope associated with the upper classes, a certain expectation that if social change is ever to come, it must be initiated by the social "haves." Sandemose's working-class protagonists have all too frequently been so broken that their potential to reform themselves is lost. Those whose humanity survives become dreamers and artists, or else build walls around themselves. The exception to this was of course Ross Dane, a protagonist that Sandemose would later disown. In many ways Claes Winckel is a strong, tolerant man. Since his authority has never been genuinely challenged, he need not assert it constantly. He selects his crew carefully, looking for mature, independent sailors of the kind that most of his fellow captains would fear: "They wanted to have weak and humble slaves on board."[14] Winckel treats his crew humanely, encouraging each member to take initiative and exercise self-judgment in difficult situations. Winckel has come a long way in suppressing the brutal, beastly side of his personality, the side which so completely dominated Adam Klinte. Yet the humane captain is a character who appears to have psychological problems. He is clearly an introverted, suppressed individual, and in keeping with this, the narrator never permits the reader to come very close to him. In one incident, Winckel appears on the deck with a rifle and quite coldly shoots down a gigantic, white seagull that had followed the "Fulton." Subsequently Winckel explains to himself why he had killed the bird: "Joy was hovering above my head, and I brought the holy ghost down with a shot. The image of joy was taken down for inspection and was a corpse."[15] The captain had seen the bird as a symbol of joy; he was therefore seized by an irresistible desire to

bring down the creature and take possession of the joy himself.
Winckel after all possesses the hunter's instinct, the desire to
seize what he wants by force. Adam Klinte abducted Anna and
enclosed her in his cabin because he saw in her the incarnation of
the love and youth of which he felt he had been deprived. Winckel
realizes the futility of such an undertaking. Shooting the bird
brings him nothing but a corpse, and above all, it represents a
terrible blow to his sense of self-worth and basic human dignity.
The act signifies failure and defeat, "--not for the sake of the
gull--who cares about it?--but for my own sake I ought not to have
done it."[16]

Winckel clearly has a need for human love, which he suppresses
and sublimates, because he is unable to cope with others on an
intimate level. On the one hand, he is undoubtedly afraid that in
an intimate relationship, his violent side will surface, as it did
when he shot the bird. This violence, which in Sandemose's work is
inevitably related to sexuality, he attempts to suppress by
imposing a meticulous order on both himself and his ship.[17]   The
outlet for his desire to possess a woman lies in possession of the
ship: "He let himself slip across the rail and entered the ship
without a sound, he felt a warmth on his hands and up between his
legs. Fulton! You have never betrayed me."[18]   As fundamental as
Winckel's fear of losing control over himself is his fear of betrayal if he were ever to become deeply involved in a relationship
with another human being. The ship represents the totally harmless
"other," an object that he can use for his own ends without at the
same time losing his human dignity.[19]   Nevertheless the ship does
not satisfy Winckel's needs. Prostitutes offer him other outlets.
He also sublimates his desire by writing a diary and making unsuccessful attempts to imitate Gullhesten's woodcarving. Nevertheless, when after a lengthy voyage the ship reaches Eskefjord in
Iceland, Winckel falls in love with Helga. In order to avoid both
the commitment and risk of failure and suffering involved in a
relationship with her, he escapes into a long illness.[20]   Ironic
but not unexpected is the fact that it is Winckel who, at the end
of the novel, commits the act of violence that brings the book to a
close. Hearing noises in the middle of the night, he leaves his
cabin and discovers that the crew members are in the process of
fleeing the ship. Desperate with anger over this betrayal, he
strikes a terrible blow at Gullhesten, who loses his balance and
tumbles on his head into the small boat waiting below.

Winckel had attempted to create a small, orderly masculine
community on board the ship. The group was committed to sail from
port to port dropping and loading its cargo. The chief antagonist
was nature; the victims of violence were rats and birds. In the
end, however, the crew lacks commitment towards the limited purpose
of Captain Winckel's society. Winckel forgets his own commitment
to self dignity, and his community explodes in a scene of violence
and death.

Gullhesten

The protagonist in Horns for Our Adornment is not Claes
Winckel, but Gullhesten, the gargantuan deck hand, who in many ways
embodies Sandemose's ideal human being: "I was too big for a
living room, I was too big for a whole factory, I was clumsy and
unlucky like an elephant. It was a strange trick on the creator's
part to make me two meters tall, and with arms like other people's
legs."[21] Symbolically as well as physically, Gullhesten is huge.
His chief purpose in life is to attain self-knowledge, and through
self-knowledge be able to control his strong, large, clumsy body.
Through self-study he also learns how to understand the people
around him and the motivations behind their often irrational and
violent acts. It is not surprising then, that Gullhesten becomes
the central figure of the "Fulton," a peacemaker whom the other
sailors love and respect.

In the first chapter of the novel Gullhesten is spending the
night with a prostitute in Bergen, who regularly offers her ser-
vices to him for nothing. After a night of sex and heavy drinking,
Gullhesten falls into a blissful daze and wishes to go to sleep:
"No, Anna, we better sleep a while now . . . ."[22] The little word
"Anna" has an explosive effect on the woman in bed next to him.
She wishes to know who Anna is, and accuses Gullhesten of betrayal.
Gullhesten never responds to the angry woman's persistent questions, but in his mind relives the painful experience of his first
love, which had taken place twenty years earlier: "She had blue
eyes. She was sixteen years old and had a dimple in her left
cheek. They were sitting one fall day in the woods. One could see
far now that the leaves were falling. She was sitting on a small
rock letting herself be worshipped. Her dress was made of blue
serge."[23]

Gullhesten had worshipped Anna, never missing an evening with
her. Only once did he fail to come to their rendezvous, because
his father was dying back home.

"One evening his father lay dying. The son was sitting by the
bed thinking of his girl.

"He closed the old man's eyes and ran. He arrived too
late."[24]

Anna, of course, had left with another man.

Slowly the suffering caused by Anna's betrayal released its
terrible grip on him, and in fact it was the pleasure he felt with
the Bergen prostitute that restored her name. The wellbeing he
feels in the soft bed evokes the bliss of stroking Anna's blue
dress twenty years earlier. His companion's brutal, jealous questioning and the rowdy scene she provokes tear Gullhesten out of his
blissful mood. After a frustrated attempt to put on his shirt, he
tears the fabric, baring his hairy chest. Then he hits the woman:

"He saw two white, shining eyes. A red light fell down from the
ceiling. It was Gullhesten who hit. He was hitting so that the
blood was gushing from her into his eyes, and he heard a crash.
Then he was fencing in empty space."[25]

In the street, and under the influence of alcohol, Gullhesten
in vain attempts to recall why he had hit the woman. Aware of his
abnormal size and strength, he vaguely senses the danger his body
presents to himself and to others unless he is able to keep it
under control. Raving down the street in the direction of the
ship, Gullhesten has a vision which will contribute to the changes
of his life: "He was grunting and humming as he walked, repeating
a line several times: Tracks of blood, blood-spattered moose
tracks! Then a name struck him, he didn't know where it came from,
but he couldn't get rid of it anymore: Gulnare! Oh Gulnare!
Beware of a man with lead in his fist!"[26] The humming voice suggests Gullhesten's basically mild nature and artistic temperament.
With his hairy chest and deep voice, he is like a goodnatured,
domesticated bear. Yet like the bear, Gullhesten is strong, and
when provoked, is capable of inflicting terrible wounds, and even
death, on his victim: "Tracks of blood, blood-spattered moose
tracks!" And as a bear-man Gullhesten offers the atavistic vision
of the Viking berserkr.[27] Moreover, since in Sandemose's work violence is most frequently sexual in origin, the victim is often a
woman: "Gulnare! Oh Gulnare! Beware of a man with lead in his
fist!" Later the cook on the ship compares Gullhesten's hand to a
hammer, thus establishing a relationship between him and the god
with the thunderbolt. Gulnare is a name Gullhesten gives to his
ideal woman in his fantasy. Incarnated as Anna, the girl in the
blue dress, or as the Bergen prostitute, she is capable of pro-
voking in him intense suffering which will sooner or later find an
outlet in violence.

During his walk from the prostitute's room back to the
"Fulton," Gullhesten has a keen sensation of his double nature, as
symbolized by his name. He is not only a berserkr, but also a
centaur, a combination of gold and horse, spirit and flesh, purity
and brute physical/sexual strength. Still in his drunken state,
Gullhesten has a second vision which points towards a solution to
his problem: "Never more shall Gulnare cry, never more shall I
sleep with her, never shall I think of her, for you have been
speaking too much, Gulnare!"[28] Gullhesten realizes that the only
way he can cope with his sexuality is by turning away from real
women, whom he considers to be treacherous, and whose words and
acts stimulate and provoke the brutal side of him (the dangerous
bear, the horse, the wolf). The insight fills him with a feeling
of profound happiness: "He laughed at his shadow, and the shadow
was a bear playing in front of him. He laughed and stretched out
his arms towards the bear. It stretched out its paws towards him
as well: You are my child, bear, a child I have brought into the
world tonight, and now I am not alone. I have given birth to a
bear while I was lying there thinking of something else."[29] His
partner will no longer be a real woman, but his own shadow, that is

a figment of his own imagination or perhaps a work of art. Back on the ship, Gullhesten will start to make up and recite brief poems, and it is not at all surprising to learn that he uses his spare time to carve out of a piece of wood a female body. The figure is complete to the slightest detail, but it lacks a head. Its name is Gulnare.

It is significant that Gulnare is headless, unable to hurt and provoke her partner through imagined words. Indeed, she is no more than a female body that Gullhesten may enjoy without struggle or guilt. She never changes. Even if he sullies her, he can simply wipe her clean and restore her to virginal purity. With the help of his headless idol, Gullhesten avoids the suffering he experienced when Anna betrayed him many years earlier. Moreover, he succeeds in taming his violently aggressive instincts. He has become an artist who has transposed a desperate need for love upon his own creation. During the stay in Iceland, Gullhesten remains the only one of the crew unaffected by the all-conquering Helga.

For Sandemose, Gullhesten is the exceptional human being: "Gullhesten was the rare combination of muscle and intelligence, and the result was a peaceful, kindly, defensive human being, without a need for either the boxer's or the thinker's fame."[30]   His natural attributes provoke others to respect him, and once he controls his sexuality through artistic sublimation, his soul and body combine into a harmonious, <u>whole</u> individual. Gullhesten is convinced that life is here and now, and he rejects any belief in an afterlife: "Something that has no meaning does not improve by being extended."[31]   His world is the one that surrounds him, and it is up to him to give it meaning. Gullhesten learns to be satisfied with what he has; jealousy and ambition are unknown concepts to him.   Consequently, he never experiences other people as his rivals, and, even when challenged, fails to strike back. This places Gullhesten in an extraordinarily independent position. Since he has no psychological need to dominate, what others think of him becomes totally irrelevant.[32]   Furthermore, he readily admits to his own weaknesses without shame. For instance, he falls victim to seasickness almost immediately after the "Fulton" has left port, but unlike the other sailors makes no attempt to hide it: "Everyone on board knew that some people had it that way, but they had never met somebody who didn't keep it a secret. 'Wait a moment while I vomit,' said Gullhesten and went over to the rail."[33]

Gullhesten's ability to admit and accept his own weaknesses enables him to tolerate the weaknesses of others. He has an unusually keen perception of their needs: "It didn't interest Gullhesten much that Bjarne was an arsonist. But since it bothered Bjarne himself, or since it bothered him that he had spoken about it, the situation was different. Gullhesten sat quietly talking a little in order to give Bjarne an opportunity to open the tumor."[34] Moreover, Gullhesten's lack of assertiveness becomes a great asset. Without seeking it, he becomes the object of adulation. Both

Bjarne and the Pastor listen with awe to what he says, even when
they only half understand his words: "The most important was that
while they were sitting there, a big and strong man was speaking
with authority. His deep and hoarse voice was vibrating among
them, even when he stopped talking. His voice was safety. It was
stronger than the man himself. It drowned out hurricanes even when
he spoke his softest. It was a blessing to have such a voice on
board."[35]

Gullhesten's chief motive in life is to learn as much as possible about himself and others. Once he has exhausted the possibilities on the "Fulton" he is seized by a compulsion to move on:
"I must see the world through new lenses. I am made that way."[36]
He therefore participates in the lot of the sailor, wandering perpetually around the world, joining one ship after the other.
Unlike the Klabautermann, however, he wanders by choice, and is not
attempting to create permanent protective walls around himself.
Ultimately, however, he too wants peace, and that is perhaps why
the narrator describes his fatal fall at the end of the novel as a
happy event: "A smile was bleeding from Gullhesten's head."[37]   In
his dying vision Gullhesten glimpses a violin: "A fiddle far away,
humming a little ditty about eternity, about the rat who finally
was permitted to enter the ship."[38]

Sandemose critics often characterize Gullhesten as a "man of
luck," the incarnation of The Flying Dutchman rather than the
Klabautermann. This interpretation is valid only if we recognize
that Gullhesten's "luck" is not necessarily bestowed upon him by
fate, but rather is a quality acquired through self-knowledge and
self-discipline. Gullhesten is a self-made man, who has chosen his
life. In this respect, he has more in common with an existentialist protagonist than with the hero of a Germanic legend or
Icelandic saga.

The Pastor

In Horns for Our Adornment Gullhesten is contrasted with the
Pastor, an incompetent, cowardly theologian who left his parish in
disgrace after the unsuccessful rape of a young girl. Lonely and
unloved, the Pastor becomes the obvious scapegoat on the "Fulton":
"When someone harassed the cook, it was out of old habit. He
quickly checked himself and boxed the ears of the Pastor, the
lightning rod, the permanently appointed Jesus."[39]   The Pastor
feels himself surrounded by enemies, a perpetual victim of the
other sailors' abuse and derisive laughter: "Everyone laughs at
me, everyone bothers me. It has always been like that. Why shall
I suffer so much? Never a friendly word. I was lying here fatally
ill. They were just laughing at me--."[40]

The Pastor is above all a weak, servile individual, whose self
image is that of a dog or worm.[41] Although he is sexually impo-
tent, his erotic desire appears boundless: "Here lay the Pastor

screaming for all members of the female sex, Jenny, Ingrid, Tora,
Ingeborg, Agnes, Vera, Tordis, Lillemor. He nagged and called on
brothers and sisters, father, mother, and everyone else, it smelled
from burned flesh after a marvelous sacrifice, while the Pastor's
mouth was making blissful smacking movements. Then he became less
cannibalistic and wanted them to live in an enclosure, he called on
the world and wanted to rule it, but the ruler unfortunately had no
following, for now he was crying for them to come. Then he cut the
matter short once more in order to rule. Finally he sneaked in
through a back door and allied himself with the Lord . . . ."[42]

The passage above shows a desperate, frustrated individual,
whose desire to dominate others is constantly thwarted. His sexual
appetite is merely a part of a more generalized desire for power.
Even his decision to become a Pastor fits into this pattern. Human
beings having failed him, he allies himself with the Almighty, who
will, he hopes, instill in him the power he so sorely desires. The
attempt is a total failure, since his career ends in a pitiful
scandal. His sexual/political appetite for power is symbolized in
the image of the tiger, which Sandemose associates with him.
According to Hareide Aarbakke, the tiger has a symbolic function[43]
similar to that of the horse, though on a more dangerous level.
It also is related to the bear which functioned as Gullhesten's
double in the opening scene of the novel, and to the wolf, which
plays such a central role in Sandemose's total work.

The Pastor's personality is revealed through his dreams. For
instance, he daydreams about romantic love and heroism, "a heart
and a cabin, spring water and the great love. The girl should have
yellow hair and mild, blue eyes, and love him a lot. He would call
her Gretchen. But it also struck him that he was destined for the
heroic, a pilot in oilskins on the outermost rock, where it was
always stormy. Or a leader of the people like Lars Oftedal, collecting the good forces in the people around him."[44]

In real life, however, his longing for love is satisfied
through an outrageous sexual act. He steals the band that Helga
wears around her braid and uses it to ornate his penis. He keeps
his fetish secret until the captain orders him to pull down his
pants to check him out for venereal disease. In similar manner,
while the Pastor is dreaming of performing heroic deeds and becoming a great leader, he is unwilling to work on transforming his
dream into reality. In fact, the Pastor has only scorn for hard,
solid labor: "They appeared to be _interested_ in this senseless
work, how did they do it? Be interested in rope, boards, tar!
They didn't have a soul."[45]

Unlike the Klabautermann, however, the Pastor's misery is of
his own making. Once during his student days, the possibility of
becoming a leader of the people had been offered to him. A young
socialist in his home town, Knut, suggested that instead of wasting
his time on studying theology, Johannes ought to become a lawyer
and assume leadership of the recently organized workers' union.

Knut was in fact paying tribute to Johannes's intellectual gifts,
and to his potential for stirring an audience. He took it for
granted that Johannes belonged in the town, and offered him a
respectable, significant place within the group: "Become a lawyer.
We need one of our own in this place. Several of us have been
speaking of it."[46]   Johannes turned down the offer without understanding the honor Knut had bestowed on him: "Others always wanted
to decide for him, others always wanted to straighten things out
for him . . . ."[47]   In fact, Johannes's refusal to become involved
in the workers' movement was based on fear: "Fear was associated
with the workers' union, he feared it like a thief fears the
police."[48]   Johannes knew that Knut and the other young workers in
the union possessed the self-confidence and sexual potency that he
himself lacked and he quenched his inferiority complex by putting
on an air of scorn toward them and the ideas they stood for. Incapable of adjusting to the _real_ world and occupy a place within a
group of _real_ people, Johannes escapes into pseudo-intellectualism:
"Johannes always became ashamed and confused whether he was
speaking to Knut or to teacher Mortensen. It was so much simpler
at the high school extension course; there they understood each
other and agreed that noble behavior paid off."[49]

Of course, Johannes' escape into abstract ideas was a failure,
and on the "Fulton" he again finds himself in the midst of a group
of genuine people. The hermetic environment on board makes the
situation doubly intolerable, and the idea of suicide and death
surfaces several times in his dream.[50]   "He was longing for a world
without light, a warm and dark world where no one could see him
clearly, and he himself only sensed the others."[51]

The Pastor's misery is directly related to his simultaneous
fear of others and his longing to be seen by them. Although he
will always attempt to hide the shameful side of himself (the
tiger), at the same time he nourishes a latent desire to be
exposed. This is illustrated in his emotions towards Gullhesten.
The Pastor senses that Gullhesten is capable of seeing through him,
and his reaction is ambivalent. On the one hand he thinks that
Gullhesten is a monstrous person, on the other he wishes that
Gullhesten's insights were yet more profound: "Once more he
thought: This person knows everything. And if it is only something he is trying to make me believe, it is because he _senses_
everything. He is a horrible person. Whoever meets a person like
that will never venture to become a Pastor. But since he understands so much, he ought to understand even more."[52]   One incident
which reveals Gullhesten's understanding of the Pastor is the episode where the giant and Claes Winckel discover Helga's band
circling the Pastor's penis. The dignified captain has only scorn
for what he sees, and orders Gullhesten to take the pantless Pastor
up to the deck and expose him to the crew. Gullhesten firmly
refuses to carry out the order, and in the end his will prevails.
The reason for Gullhesten's compassion is again his self-knowledge;
he has recognized within himself traits which surface in exag-
gerated fashion in the Pastor. Most importantly, Gullhesten is

aware of the "horse" side of his personality, and his understanding has enabled him to neutralize it and consequently render it harmless. On the other hand the Pastor has never been able to resolve the problem of the "tiger" within him. As a result, he exists in constant misery, frustrated, scorned, and ridiculed. His predominant longing for a dark world where no one can see him forms a stark contrast to Gullhesten's love of light. Gullhesten quotes lines from poems about the sun, and even in his dying vision, light dominates the darkness: "He tumbled down into the darkness, but the fall was loaded with light."

Nevertheless, the Pastor does have occasional glimpses of self-awareness. Once, after a gigantic drinking party on the ship, he has a nightmare about the tiger and starts screaming wildly. His cries awaken the rest of the crew members, but they quickly go back to sleep again.[53] The Pastor is left with his own thoughts: "The Pastor had been thinking strange thoughts while lying there bitterly alone with his fear: One day I shall become friends with the Tiger.

"He saw himself on a speaker's chair above an ocean of people. Next to him lay the Tiger looking at the crowd."[54] To become friends with the tiger, to accept his double nature, would indeed be a gigantic step towards resolving his psychological problem. In his vision the Pastor addresses a huge crowd. His desire for power and domination over others, it appears, has not disappeared, and consequently the problem is far from resolved. More hopeful, perhaps, is the glimpse of awareness he has during a time of illness that sexual insufficiency lies at the root of his misery. During a clear moment in the midst of a fever delirium, the Pastor orders Gullhesten, who is sitting by his side reading the Old Testament, to "cut it off."[55] At first Gullhesten believes that the other is referring to the ropes that are tying the unruly sick man to his bed. However, it immediately becomes clear to him that the Pastor is pleading for castration, since he senses that sexuality has become the controlling factor in his life: "Gullhesten became stiff in the face and didn't move a finger. But the Pastor lay perfectly still and said no more.

"Then Gullhesten sensed something strange in the silence, a wave between himself and the other."[56] Aware that the Pastor's problem is similar to what he himself had once experienced, Gullhesten nevertheless cannot assist his companion. While Gullhesten was strong enough to tame his "horse" side, the Pastor is too weak to cope with the tiger that resides within him. In spite of Gullhesten's attempts to befriend him and to protect him from the other sailors, the Pastor remains a pathetic character from beginning to end. Instead of facing his problem head on, and by so doing attempt to resolve it, he chooses evasion by dreaming of changing his environment: "One day I may find something else, a place where no one knows me? In America?"[57] The reader, of course, recognizes that what needs to undergo change is not the environment but rather the Pastor himself.

In Horns for Our Adornment, the narrator's point of view has clearly changed. It is as if the confrontation with Jante in A Fugitive Crosses His Tracks had given Sandemose a new perspective. Life on board the "Fulton" is very different from that on the "Ariel," or for that matter from life in Jante itself. Fear of others, which had paralyzed so many of Sandemose's earlier protagonists, has lost some of its sting. In one of the many digressions inserted within the narrative thread of the novel, a father gives his son the following piece of advice: "If you are afraid you must never run away until you are completely sure of what you fear."[58] Moreover, the root of human anguish is most frequently to be found within the individual himself, rather than in any specific outside source. Inner strength is the key to peace. Gullhesten is not destined to be a "man of luck"; nor is the Pastor destined to be an outcast. Each man chooses his own essence in true existentialist fashion.

The following citation illustrates the road Sandemose's narrator has covered since Tales from Labrador: "There was a feeble light far ahead. The road was difficult. A brook flowed through a crevice. I felt the cold water in my shoes. I climbed over slippery rocks and could not see.

"Then I broke through. Ahead of me was a plain, and beyond it an enormous mountain. The mountain turned all its faces towards me. I took a deep breath. Finally I saw the holy mountain from all its sides.

"It was morning. The sun set the sky above the mountain on fire. I was thinking: here lives a purified humanity."[59]

No longer the chained slave looking at Halfway Mountain from one single point of view, the narrator in Horns for Our Adornment has a full, open view: "The mountain turned all its sides towards me." The ending of the novel appears unduly optimistic. In spite of Gullhesten's death, images of light, purification, and rejuvenation prevail. In a final vision, the narrator sees a young woman lying in the grass. When he reaches her, she opens her eyes and says to him: "I told them that I would not continue without you. Then I was permitted to stay for the time being. All those who possess the dream of a purified humanity will awaken one day at the gate of heaven."[60] The woman gets up and the two stand facing each other: "All our thoughts were like a golden fog around us. I didn't grasp her. It made me wonder feebly, and then she smiled."[61]

In all of Sandemose's works so far, male sexuality is considered a brutal force, "horns" with which characters like big John Wakefield used to ornate themselves. Two of the characters in the Beaver Coulee novels tried to tame their sexuality through marriage and the founding of home and family. In A Fugitive Crosses His Tracks, the Jante law attempts to legislate restrictions upon the natural growth of human beings, and the result is catastrophic.

Outwardly taboo, sexuality actually became the central focus of
Jante. In The Klabautermann sexuality was given free rein, and the
novel ended in a huge shipwreck. The crew members in Horns for our
Adornment are more restrained than Adam Klinte and Gösta Porajärvi,
and the marriage option appears not to be open to them. Instead of
constantly undermining each other in the fashion of Jante, they
make use of fetishes to help them cope with their frustration (the
carved statue of Gulnare, Helga's silver band). More significantly
perhaps, Gullhesten is the first Sandemose character who bridles
his eroticism and need for power by placing primary emphasis upon
self-knowledge through introspection. It is interesting that
artistic creation becomes a significant support in his struggle to
find peace.

Horns for Our Adornment marks a significant step forward for
Sandemose's narrator. Far from having reached the end of the
tunnel, he is nevertheless starting to perceive light ahead. In
the final vision of the novel, the young woman extends a promise to
the young man: "All those who possess the dream of a purified
humanity, will awaken one day at the gate of heaven." The narrator
does possess this dream, and he has pointed out a way to transform
the dream into reality. Gullhesten does attempt to make life more
livable on board the "Fulton." Nevertheless, he remained basically
a loner to the end, he never attempted to rid himself of his restless sailor's nature, and the peace he finds is ultimately the
peace of death. The only thing he ever builds is the headless
statue of Gulnare. It is therefore not surprising that the narrator, after having built up, even idealized his protagonist, will in
the end admit that Gullhesten's solution is a mere step ahead at
best. Gullhesten has succeeded in taming the beast within himself,
but he is never willing to confront and resolve the problem of his
relationship to women. This he would have to do in order to become
a true social builder. As it is, his role in the building of a new
society is limited to that of peacemaker. In the end, he shows
himself more committed to himself than to the group. The narrator
remedies Gullhesten's failure somewhat by reintegrating woman into
his own vision at the end of the novel. He perceives the young
woman in the grass neither as the traditional, supportive wife, nor
as a madonna or whore, but as an equal partner on the road through
life. The final sentence in Horns for Our Adornment clearly points
in this direction: "We [the young woman and the young man] went
side by side across the plain, towards the gate in the holy
mountain."[62]

Notes

1. Blaise Pascal, Pensées, edited by Leon Brunschvicg. Paris: Nelson Editeurs, 1955, p. 151.

2. Verker i utvalg, IV, p. 212. See Hallberg, The Icelandic Saga, p. 83.

3. Verker i utvalg, IV, p. 182.

4. Ibid., p. 192. Sandemose's italics.

5. Ibid., p. 288.

6. Ibid., p. 281.

7. Ibid., p. 304.

8. Ibid., p. 282.

9. Ibid., p. 297.

10. Ibid., p. 164. The Klabautermann legend frequently associates the spirit with various animals, most notably rats. See Buss, The Klabautermann of the Northern Sea, p. 43.

11. Verker i utvalg, IV, p. 168.

12. In Saint-Genêt Sartre discusses how the image others have of us influences our self-image. See Saint-Genêt, pp. 14-15.

13. Verker i utvalg, IV, p. 145.

14. Ibid., p. 148.

15. Ibid., p. 195.

16. Ibid.

17. Ibid., p. 212.

18. Ibid., p. 143.

19. For an extensive discussion of the relationship between the self and others, see Sartre, L'Etre et le néant, pp. 265-481.

20. In Existentialist literature the characters frequently escape into illness in order to avoid situations they feel incapable of handling.

21. Verker in utvalg, IV, p. 127.

22. Ibid., p. 122.

23. Ibid., p. 124.

24. Ibid., p. 125. Sandemose's italics.

25. Ibid., p. 124.

26. Ibid., p. 126.

27. This in turn brings to mind Montague Summers' connection
between the wolf-man and the bear-man: "In modern Scandinavia the
term is varúlf, which has been extended to include the
shapeshifting to a bear, for of all the hamrammir none were more
famous than the berserkir, the bear-sark men." Montague Summers,
The Werewolf, p. 242.

28. Verker i utvalg, IV, p. 127.

29. Ibid.

30. Ibid., p. 174.

31. Ibid., p. 266.

32. Ibid., p. 238.

33. Ibid., p. 152.

34. Ibid., p. 236.

35. Ibid., pp. 282-83.

36. Ibid., p. 297.

37. Ibid., p. 305.

38. Ibid.

39. Ibid., p. 183.

40. Ibid., p. 197.

41. Ibid., pp. 296, 298.

42. Ibid., p. 175.

43. Høyt på en vinget hest, p. 124.

44. Verker i utvalg, IV, p. 153.

45. Ibid.

46. Ibid., p. 201.

47. Ibid.

48. Ibid., p. 198.

49. Ibid.

50. Høyt på en vinget hest, pp. 248-49.

51. Verker i utvalg, IV, p. 249.

52. Ibid. Sandemose's italics.

53. The incident is reminiscent of the story in the Bible where the disciples are sleeping during Christ's agonizing struggle with himself.

54. Verker i utvalg, IV, p. 236.

55. The expression "cut it off" derives from the Bible, where in St. Matthew, XVIII, 8, one can read: "Wherefore if thy hand or thy foot offend thee, cut them off, and cast them from thee: it is better for thee to enter into life halt or maimed, rather than having two hands or two feet to be cast into everlasting fire."

56. Verker i utvalg, IV, p. 177.

57. Ibid., p. 273. See pp. 283-84. The human tendency to escape problems rather than resolving them is discussed at length throughout the work of Sartre. The French author calls it "mauvaise foi" or "bad faith." See for example L'Etre et le néant, pp. 82-107.

58. Verker i utvalg, IV, p. 234.

59. Ibid., p. 306.

60. Ibid. Sandemose's italics.

61. Ibid., p. 307.

62. Ibid.

6.
September: Towards a New Moral Code

    September is the last of Sandemose's novels about the
Scandinavian immigrant community in Beaver Coulee. The time is
autumn 1939, with the outbreak of World War II functioning as a
backdrop for the personal crises of the protagonists. The themes
of personal crisis and the approaching war are intertwined,
ultimately merging when several of the main characters perish as
their ship returning to Norway is sunk in the middle of the
Atlantic.

    While the setting is Beaver Coulee, the character gallery is
once again modified. Most significantly, Ross Dane and Espen
Arnakke have disappeared. The new protagonist is Røde Fane (Red
Flag), a Dutch immigrant, one of Espen Arnakke's friends in A
Sailor Goes Ashore. The female protagonist, Vera Tynset, is a new
settler. With her husband, Emil, and young son, Per, she has
bought the farm of Sten and Maja Eriksen, who have parted from the
community and settled in San Francisco. The transfer of the prop-
erty is important, since Vera and Emil are Maja and Sten in new
dress.

    As the novel opens, Røde Fane is approaching the Tynset farm
to make inquiries about purchasing a horse. He finds Vera home
alone, and as the two meet in the kitchen, they experience a passionate sexual attraction. They make love on the spot, and the
incident initiates a powerful affair. Rumors about them start cir-
culating in Beaver Coulee, and an anonymous letter revealing the
matter reaches Emil. His instinctive reaction is to kill Røde
Fane, but he is unable to carry out the plan. Instead he yields to
Vera's desire to leave Canada and return to Norway, where he is
determined to divorce his wife. As World War II erupts, the family

embarks on a perilous Atlantic crossing. On the day Vera commits
suicide by leaping into the ocean, the other passengers perish as
the ship is torpedoed. Back in Beaver Coulee, Vera's uncle Frans
and old Pedersen, one of the original settlers left in Beaver
Coulee, die. Heartbroken, Røde Fane decides against an earlier
wish to return to Holland. He remains on the farm with Pedersen's
son, Fredrik.

Sexuality and the Traditional Family Structure

   September is above all a novel about sexuality. It questions
both the patriarchal family structure and conventional conjugal
fidelity. It disassociates sexual abstinence from the concept of
female purity. In his description of Vera Tynset, Sandemose
develops a female character type which he earlier had sketched in
his portrait of Maja Eriksen in A Sailor Goes Ashore; and he will
develop the type fully in his complex treatment of Felicia in The
Werewolf.

   When Røde Fane and Vera meet in the Tynset kitchen, they completely lose control over their acts: "Røde Fane could never
explain to himself what had happened in that moment. For something
happened, whatever it was, it was as if he staggered internally,
put the brakes on hard . . . and afterwards he remembered that she
had tilted her lips a little backwards - like the mare's blissful,
hellish grin when the stallion arrives with flying mane . . . .

   "And she resembled a young mare, on her slender legs, her
large, shy eyes, and her arched breast which was to make him close
his hands each time he thought of it."[1] The description brings to
mind the horse symbolism in A Fugitive Crosses His Path and Horns
for Our Adornment. It conjures up as well the description in A
Sailor Goes Ashore, when Bodilsen's stallion attacks Sten Eriksen's
mare and kills her. Before dying, however, the mare castrates and
destroys her attacker. A major difference, however, between the
scene including Vera and Røde Fane and those of earlier novels lies
in the fact that formerly unbridled eroticism was seen by Sandemose
as a destructive force. The partners literally wipe each other
out. Moreover, Sandemose emphasized the unequal size of the
adversaries. In Horns for Our Adornment sexuality was an inner
force that Gullhesten had to suppress in order to live a harmonious
life. On the other hand, in September Røde Fane and Vera take
pleasure in their sexuality. Their union is seen as a joyous,
amazing occurrence and Røde Fane is laughing into the air as he
leaves the farm. Above all, the two are physically and emotionally
equal. Vera is a tall, strong woman, in every way Røde Fane's
match.

   Retrospectively, however, Røde Fane commences to associate
eroticism with transgression. Vera's laughter reminds him of hell.
Moreover, the image of the mating horses underscores the bestial
quality of the sex act. While brushing aside the problem of

personal guilt: --"There had been no time for guilt"[2]--Røde Fane instinctively condemns women who make themselves sexually available, and he attempts to convince himself that Vera is different: "It was obvious that that kind of thing otherwise never happened at the Tynset farm."[3] Røde Fane, to whom the narrator refers as a "young and lonely <u>wolf</u>,"[4] has received his name because of his unwillingness to marry and settle down: "Therefore he had become the evil element in this moral land, for he wasn't made for a life of abstinence."[5] Once falling in love with Vera, however, he has no higher wish than to give up his freedom. He dreams of marrying her, for she symbolizes to him joy, friendship, and home, "a place where he would be happy to enter when the day was finished."[6] He starts thinking of Vera's family as if it were his own, of her young son Per as his child. Røde Fane's view of sexuality and love, then, turns quite conventional. Once in love with Vera, he wants her to belong to <u>him</u> alone, and he would like to construct the protective walls of marriage and family around her, her child, and himself.

Røde Fane is a typical Sandemose outsider. He originally came to Canada from Holland "because they were pestering him to death because of a child he had fathered, and he was unable to provide for himself; there wasn't a day's work to be found. He had been chased away from his homeland like a mangy dog."[7] He retains strong emotional ties to his native country to which he dreams of returning. However, he has no family and no real ties to Holland. What he longs for appears to be a vaguely defined "homeland."

Vera's situation is different: "She belonged to a family that had been economically independent for centuries, she possessed the courage and honesty which old money provides."[8] As a member of the old farming aristocracy, she has deep roots in Norway; yet she had willingly followed her husband to Canada. Unlike Røde Fane, who felt that he had been driven away from Holland, Vera knows that her family wants her to remain. Since she is an <u>insider</u>, the word <u>home</u> has little of the mythic quality that it has for Røde Fane and all those who feel that they had never possessed it: "Vera had built a nest at the new place like a migrating bird. She was the kind of person who cannot stand moving, but settles down anywhere, as long as she is together with those she loves."[9] Largely because of her secure origins, Vera is psychologically at peace with herself. Never deprived nor mistreated, unscarred by "Jante," she bears no social grudges. As long as she has Emil and Per, she is tranquil in Beaver Coulee. Conversely, when she realizes that she has lost them, she insists on leaving the place and returning to Norway.

Vera's marriage to Emil appears to be a happy one, built upon the principle of equality. The two go hunting together; frankness and openness are the norm in the home. Her physical size is the same as that of her husband. Røde Fane underscores Vera's masculine beauty. In fact, he finds Vera so attractive because she is not the conventional male standard of femininity: "She is a kind of boy."[10]

Vera's view of sexuality is unorthodox. Her adventure with
Røde Fane was a spontaneous, joyous event, that engenders no
feeling of guilt for her. She mothers her lover, and she thinks of
their relationship as an occurrence compatible with her love for
Emil. Above all, she fails to understand that her affair with Røde
Fane ought to deprive Emil of anything: "It had been fun, and no
one had lost anything."[11] Instinctively, Vera wishes to inform
Emil of what has happened but refrains from doing so out of fear of
a jealous reaction. Vera's concerns are thoroughly justified.
Having read the anonymous letter informing him about his wife's
conduct, he takes a gun and intends to kill Røde Fane. Instead of
using the weapon, however, he breaks down and informs his rival of
his belief that Vera is innocent: "She is so good, so innocent.
It means nothing to her. She would think she was the same, even if
. . . even if there had been a hundred. She thinks I am insane,
because I take it this way. She is so innocent, as if she doesn't
know . . . she only smiles. Smiles."[12] Because she has no sense
of having done anything wrong, Vera is innocent. Aware of this,
Emil accepts her childlike spontaneity. Nevertheless, his
jealousy, his desire to possess her, prevails. Far from diminishing, Emil's jealousy becomes more intense as he ruminates over
the events in his own mind. The situation reaches its climax when,
on the ship, he asks Vera whether he is indeed Per's father. At
this point, Vera submits to feelings of guilt, not so much because
of her relationship with Røde Fane, but because she has broken her
husband: "I have done that, I have broken Emil, and therefore it
was wrong. She had no other consciousness of sin, but it broke her
down. Now she felt as if there was only an external shell left.
Inside everything had collapsed."[13]

The conventional morality of others led Vera to suicide. Røde
Fane sums up what has happened at the end of the novel: "Vera was
dead. She had accepted her punishment for being what she was. She
didn't exterminate herself because she went astray, not because she
was sinning, but in order to liberate others from something they
didn't understand, so as to spare them the sorrow that she was like
that and was doing things they could never imagine doing."[14] Torn
by grief and guilt, Røde Fane cries openly in front of Fredrik,
who, in an instant of insight, (perhaps the only one in his whole
life), tries to console him by saying that in any confrontation
there is never only one guilty party. Indeed, because he refused
to forgive his wife, Emil must share Røde Fane's guilt. Moreover,
Emil's chief motivation was sexual jealousy, which he permitted to
control him even when he fully realized that Vera's morality was
different from his own, and that his love for her had been stimulated by the fact that she was different.

Nevertheless, for Sandemose the chief culprit in the tragedy
is the community--with its intolerance, maliciousness, and thirst
for gossip. Once more, it is "Jante" that has been transplanted on
to the Canadian prairie. Even in a land where, in a sense, every
individual is an exile, the group must seek out convenient scape-
goats. The scapegoat need not be an ethnic outsider. In fact, the

most vicious intolerance is directed against non-conformists within the Scandinavian community. In A Sailor Goes Ashore Sten and Maja were harassed because they had failed to fit, and ultimately we learn that they did leave the community. Emil and Vera must flee their farm in the middle of the night in order to avoid overt mob scenes against the "faithless wife."

In many ways, Vera represents the liberated woman, who has avoided entrapment in a predominantly male image of herself. Vera is natural and androgynous; she fails to relate sexuality with sin. She refuses to serve as a prize between jealous male rivals. In the end she is broken only through realization that her acts and attitudes have deeply hurt the people about whom she cares most. She is an innocent victim of a less-than-perfect environment.

A Voice of Moderation

Sandemose's chief spokesman in September may be neither Vera, Røde Fane, nor Emil, but the communist, Vilfred Larsen, another minor character from A Sailor Goes Ashore. In September Vilfred and his adopted son Jim are still living in Beaver Coulee. Vilfred is a convenient target for the wrath of the settlers, who believe it is improper for a man to adopt a child. However, Vilfred is impervious to the criticism, he chooses confrontation rather than pick up his belongings and leave. Røde Fane explains that Vilfred manages to endure peace with a hostile group because he never becomes involved in other people's affairs: "He didn't need women either--in any case not so much that it was in any way distracting--and all in all he didn't need many tangible things. In the evening he was sitting with a book, or looking with interest at the wall, or repairing Jim's clothes while whistling a song.

"Vilfred was a cold fire. That's how one ought to be. Observe what people were doing, but not participate oneself."[15] When Vilfred sits staring at the wall in the evening, he likely is meditating upon the new society that he hopes to help construct. We know relatively little about Vilfred's Marxist utopia, except that it is a place where men and women are equal, and where concern for the child is more important than personal sexual gratification. For Vilfred, erotic freedom simply is irrelevant: "The male had forgotten that in one woman he had them all, and the female had forgotten the same unchanging truth, that one man is all men . . . God knows how long woman must be free before she settles down in her freedom, and before the male recognizes the liberated woman as the mother."[16] In other words, men must stop turning women into idols (The Holy Mother) and start treating them as equal partners.

According to Vilfred, contemporary society is in a chaotic, transitional state, coinciding with the degree of erotic liberation. Having broken out of a state where childbearing and rearing were considered her only function, the modern woman tends to discard her traditional function altogether in order to indulge her

newly won sexual freedom. According to Vilfred, however, the liberated couple of the future will realize that all sexual partners
have little to distinguish them, and, out of consideration for
their children, should be satisfied with one another. Interestingly enough, once Vera understands that she must choose between,
on the one hand, Røde Fane, and on the other, Emil and Per, she
never hesitates. Moreover, once she discovers that she has
destroyed Emil's confidence in her, and consequently both her marriage and family, her will to live disappears.

The drama in Beaver Coulee is played out against the backdrop
of approaching war and destruction. As in The Klabautermann, and
in spite of Vera's innocence and goodness, unbridled sexuality
leads to chaos and death. Vera, Emil, and Per die untimely deaths.
A question Sandemose poses in September is: Why do people refuse
one another forgiveness, when they all are at the mercy of forces
they cannot control,--namely sexual drives, illness, and war? Why
do they remain set in their destructive ways even while observing
conventions that lead to misery and destruction? According to
Fredrik Pedersen: "We turn life into hell for one another because
no one dares run a risk."[17] The most positive thought emerging
from the novel is that even people like Fredrik can learn. Having
spent his life in competition with his father collecting money and
wealth, an individual who even made an attempt on his father's
life, Fredrik is human after all. He finds words of consolation
for Røde Fane, and proposes to him a union of lonely people: "He
stopped, as if the sentence had been cut off with a pair of scis-
sors, and said in a low voice that no one had ever heard from Fred
Coyote, the prairie wolf--a voice which was rusty with emotion:
"I'm alone . . . well Fane kid, let's go and have something to
eat!"[18] Once again, then, the solution proposed to a heterosexual
love story is a union between two men.

The Collapse of the Dream of Beaver Coulee

September is the last of Sandemose's Beaver Coulee novels, and
it marks his disillusionment with establishing a model community in
the new world. No character in September possesses faith in and
enthusiasm for Ross Dane's vision. When Røde Fane inherits one of
old Pedersen's farms, rather than cultivate it, he sells it to the
first bidder for a ridiculous price. Fredrik Pedersen still likes
to accumulate as much land as possible, and does invite Røde Fane
to join him at the end of the book. Unfortunately, because neither
man has any sense of responsibility to the community at large,
their union is unproductive. The settlers in Beaver Coulee are
restless and unstable. In face of the slightest adversity, they
are anxious to abandon their farms. Ever present is the dream of
forsaking Alberta and return to Europe: "Several farms already lay
waste,--and so the owners left them whether they wanted to or not.
It didn't pay to stay. One was unfaithful towards the earth, but
one day would surely come when it would take its revenge. Was the
conquest of the earth to be a pillage? It wasn't only that they

systematically dried up a whole continent, they had become root-
less. One often heard a farmer say: When we get older and have
enough to leave.

"They didn't leave. They stayed and handed over the
impoverished soil to their children. Some had made money but all
had lost another kind of wealth, a wealth whose existence they
didn't recognize until it was gone: They lived without resonance,
in an indifferent place where no stone was whispering to them: Can
you remember the time when you were picking flowers here, while
your father was sawing down the big pine tree?"[19]

Sandemose's narrator is echoing Knut Hamsun's idea of the soil
as the only dependable value, and of faithfulness towards the earth
as the one guarantee for a peaceful, happy life. Recognizing the
need for emigration, based on the failure of the poor to survive in
old Europe--"for if one could not acquire food there was nothing,
not even a homeland"[20] --, Sandemose regrets that the recent generation of pioneers was unable to put down roots in the new land. Instead of developing loyalty to the rich Canadian prairie, the immigrants limited their goals to making sufficient money to leave. By
way of contrast, old Ross Dane never for an instant contemplated
parting from Beaver Coulee. This souring of the narrator's attitude towards the immigrant experience made it quite predictable
that Sandemose's next work should have a location in Scandinavia,
not the Denmark which he had forever left behind, but rather
Norway, his mother's homeland, which he had chosen as his own in
1929.

Notes

1. Aksel Sandemose, <u>September</u>, Copenhagen: Det Schønbergske Forlag, 1976, pp. 11-12. Sandemose's italics.

2. <u>Ibid</u>., p. 13.

3. <u>Ibid</u>.

4. <u>Ibid</u>., p. 26.

5. <u>Ibid</u>.

6. <u>Ibid</u>., p. 52.

7. <u>Ibid</u>., p. 36.

8. <u>Ibid</u>., p. 68.

9. <u>Ibid</u>., p. 36.

10. <u>Ibid</u>., p. 10.

11. <u>Ibid</u>., p. 68.

12. <u>Ibid</u>., p. 102.

13. <u>Ibid</u>., p. 134.

14. <u>Ibid</u>., p. 155.

15. <u>Ibid</u>., p. 113.

16. <u>Ibid</u>., p. 104.

17. <u>Ibid</u>., p. 85.

18. <u>Ibid</u>., p. 157. Sandemose's italics.

19. <u>Ibid</u>., p. 35.

20. <u>Ibid</u>.

7.

The Past Is a Dream:
Survival through Art

The Past Is a Dream is undoubtedly Sandemose's most successful novel, a complex, psychologically convincing, rigorously composed work, whose themes and characters are complementary according to a principle of reflecting mirrors.

The central theme concerns the moral and psychological collapse of the protagonist, John Torson, which is played against the backdrop of the collapse of Norway before the German invasion of April 1940. The central idea is whether the country and protagonist will survive their parallel crises without permanent damage. Will John Torson, for example, be forced to resort to a radical solution similar to that chosen by Audun Hamre, the protagonist of The Tar Dealer, who destroyed himself and his fortress. The narrator realizes the difficulty of his struggle: "One knew that before this could be restored, if it could be restored, one had to live many years, and fight, fight against the stupidity and evil in oneself and others."[1]

In certain ways The Past Is a Dream bears a striking resemblance to Johan Borgen's Lillelord trilogy. Both novels conclude when it becomes clear that the Germans have lost the war; in both novels, the forces of national survival prevail. The protagonists differ, however. While "Lillelord"--Vilfred Sagen--collaborates with the enemy and becomes progressively defeatist, John Torson never completely abandons his struggle to retain a measure of self-respect: "We do not want to live if the Germans should win this war!"[2] the narrator states. A commitment to his art, which Vilfred did not possess, ultimately saves John. Consumed with self-hatred, Borgen's protagonist joined the enemy and committed suicide on the day of national liberation. Both Vilfred and John discovered during World War II that their enemies were the primitive, destructive forces within their own selves. According to the narrator in The Past Is a Dream: "Nature is our enemy, it is against all that is called humanity and culture."[3] Both Vilfred and John find guilt. According to Asmund Lien, "The reconstructed image of his own 'I' can only fill him [John Torson] with scorn."[4] Nevertheless, Vilfred loses his battle, while John survives by virtue of turning his inner experience into a work of art. Even so, the ending of The Past Is a Dream is far from optimistic. Ultimately the narrator feels the words he writes on paper may serve no purpose. In the final lines of the book, the narrator compares himself to a Prometheus who, unlike the archetypal hero, is ultimately unable to benefit mankind: "I wandered around for centuries, but never did I find the path which Prometheus followed when he brought down the flame from the holy mountain. I have no flame, I have nothing to tell you, I have nothing to give you, and now he is touching my shoulder to tell me that the boat a ready to depart."[5] While one can certainly identify the ship as Charon's, about to ferry John Torson into the realm of death, it is of course equally possible that Torson's departure signals simply a new stage on the road of life.

The Plot

In 1939 John (né Johannes) Torson, returns to Norway for an eighteen-month visit after an absence of thirty-one consecutive years in the United States. At fifty, John is a successful industrialist, owning a large tool factory and a comfortable home in San Francisco. The motive for Torson's trip is nostalgic, a desire to find Agnes, the sweetheart of his youth who had betrayed him years before. Torson wishes to resume his relationship with her. He wishes to buy her back, and turn an old defeat into victory.

The day following John's arrival in Oslo, newspapers carry the sensational story of violent death that has just occurred in the garden of Torson's ancestral home in the village of Gjørstad. According to reports, one Anton Strand had entered the garden with a gun, presumably with the intention of killing John's younger brother, Karl Manfred. The latter seemingly was Anton's rival for the love of Jenny Lund, who lives in the house with her grandfather who now owns it. During the moments preceding the killing, Karl Manfred and Jenny had been sitting together in the living room. Jenny left the room briefly, Karl Manfred went outside through another door, a shot was fired in the garden, and shortly afterwards Anton Strand was found dead, a loaded pistol in his hand. In spite of Karl Manfred's persistent pleas of innocence, he was accused of manslaughter, found guilty, and sentenced to a year in prison.

John Torson takes an obvious interest in the strange case, which he promises himself to resolve. He visits Gjørstad and meets Jenny, who falls in love with him. Though John's feelings toward the woman are cooler, the two enjoy a brief affair and Jenny becomes pregnant. While at Gjørstad, John also catches a glimpse of Agnes, who, as a result of poverty and frequent childbearing, is prematurely haggard. Returning to Oslo, John meets the writer Gunder Gundersen and his wife, Susanne. In Susanne, John sees the reincarnation of the Agnes of his youth, and he becomes passionately infatuated with her. Despite Jenny, despite Gunder who loves his wife and considers John his friend, and despite Gullan, Susanne's small daughter, John and Susanne have a tumultuous love affair. After several months, however, John, who fears to be tied down, breaks off the relationship and returns to San Francisco. The date is September 1940. In the meantime Hitler has occupied Norway.

Back home in San Francisco, John spends his nights attempting to organize the rambling diary he kept during his year and a half in Norway. The rewriting takes the form of a reflective voyage, a long journey into the narrator's self: "It is a description of an internal voyage, with words that are chosen and weighed so that they could be used on something I believed to be nothing, to give a name to something I do not know."[6] John's genuine exploration of the past, then, takes place during this second trip, the phase of naming rather than experiencing. As he receives a wire informing him that Jenny has given birth to his son and namesake, John decides to turn his writing into a letter to the boy. He intends to have his son receive it after his death. The Past Is a Dream, then, is presented as the narrator's testament. It is also a dialogue with the self, an attempt for John Torson to structure the events of the past, and in so doing, understand and free himself from them.

John starts writing because he feels confused and guilty. The purpose of his work is to explain and justify his life. By so doing he hopes to attain freedom. John's writing, however, has an unexpected effect. Far from offering a catharsis, the strokes of John's pen accentuate his guilt. Not only is there evidence to suggest that he may himself be the murderer of Anton Strand, but he also indicts himself in other tragedies--the deaths of Susanne and Karl Manfred, the insanity of Gunder Gundersen, and the death of Mary Brooke, one of his former female friends. In the manner of Oedipus, it is the self-appointed detective who, paradoxically, turns out to be the criminal.

One may justifiably note the similarities between John Torson and previous Sandemose protagonists. Espen Arnakke in A Sailor Goes Ashore left Scandinavia because he felt grossly mistreated by society; John left because of Agnes's betrayal. Like Espen, John planned to make a fortune in the new world, then return and punish the hometown skeptics. Each felt like an outcast determined to change his fate, a "Klabautermann" wishing to become "The Flying Dutchman," a Thor wishing to become a Christ, a "man without luck" wishing to become a "man of luck." While Espen never returns to Jante, John literally realizes his fantasy. In fact, his very name encompasses the two sides of his personality. Thor is the outcast, the "hammer man" or Klabautermann. John, on the other hand, carries the heritage of John Wakefield, the "man of luck," the individual who succeeded in taking Eva away from Espen in Misery Harbor. Thus Sandemose's new protagonist represents John and Thor welded together, in other words, a more complete human being than any of Sandemose's previous protagonists.

John left Norway because Agnes was unfaithful to him. For thirty-one years he pondered this most humiliating defeat of his life, and never abandoned hope of reversing the situation. Agnes herself proves to be a disappointment, but during his stay in Norway John is determined to play the role of the conqueror. Thus, he takes Jenny from Karl Manfred, and Susanne from Gunder, a vengeance of sorts upon Røde Henrik, who had taken Agnes away from him a generation earlier. Asmund Lien points out, quite correctly, that "John Torson's relationship to women is completely dead when he perceives no rival."[8] The reason for this is of course that John Torson has an urgent psychological need, not to love a woman, but to conquer his rivals. Moreover, John quickly discovers that he is more powerful than Røde Henrik ever was since he has at his disposal a dreadful weapon, namely a huge amount of money. Because of his wealth people will gather around him and willingly take his side: "I have told how I read scorn in many eyes when people discovered what was happening between Susanne and me. Still we had willing helpers when Gunder broke down. I could pay bills at Cafe Hjørnet, one could borrow money from me, and Gunder had many enemies to whom Susanne handed him over without second thought. But most of all it was because people didn't like to be on unfriendly terms with the rich man."[9] His symbolic victory over his rivals is sealed when, after Karl Manfred's death, John gains control over the entire family heritage.

In the long run, however, John's apparent strength turns out to be a liability, since it gradually corrupts his personality. His material success was built upon his commitment to a vision of the past, to his all-consuming goal of regaining Agnes. This faithfulness, which ultimately represents faithfulness to an illusion, has made John unable or unwilling to establish meaningful relationships with others. The central message he wants to convey to his son is to beware of false visions. "You shall not be true to a vision. It leads you to the abyss. But how can I teach you to betray your vision? You shall be true to the living person, keep away from old mental ruins! But how can I teach you that?"[10] In fact, through his absolute faithfulness to his dream of Agnes, John has become a traitor to the rest of humanity. The parallel to Scott Fitzgerald's The Great Gatsby is striking.

Time

The period during which John reorganizes his diary is from September 1940 to May 1944, while Norway suffers under the occupation. On the other hand, the narrator appears to have found peace. He has emerged beyond the agony and restlessness of the diary's author and is living on a different plane of consciousness: "What was it that I wrote in this book: 'Love and murder are the only things worth writing about.' That is not true, nothing is worth writing about. The only thing of value is silence, to sit in the great silence and listen to it, without any desire."[11] The narrator cherishes his long, quiet, solitary nights in San Francisco, poring over his manuscripts in an attempt to impose order on his rambling notes. The soundless clock on the wall testifies that he is experiencing time differently now. The hands of the clock moving noiselessly in seemingly endless circles fail to interfere with his introspection: "Twelve hours had passed before I rose from my chair. When lifting my face I saw the large second hand floating silently on the face of the clock."[12] This contemplative experience contrasts sharply with John's enslavement to the clock prior to his visit to Norway: "My day had for many years been a workday accurately divided up from when I got up until I went to bed."[13] Clearly John has moved away from an experience of "public" time, which Meyerhoff tells us that "we use, with the aid of watches, calendars, etc., in order to synchronize our private experiences of time for the purpose of social action and communication," towards a contemplative state, which "can be achieved only through a liberation from time, craving, and personality."[14]

The trip, of course, had provoked a radical break in John's routine, a break which would contribute to bringing him to the point of psychological crisis: "I knew that I had experienced such disturbances before, but I could not remember when. The whole thing irritated me. It was this life of leisure that I didn't tolerate."[15] The war in Europe is clearly of less significance to John than his own private life. During the eighteen months in the country he had left three decades earlier, the past intrudes upon the present in a way far different from the days of his orderly life in San Francisco. Above all, he senses keenly that a large block of time has passed: "Once more I wonder, as I have done so often, about the road I have covered. I measured the distance at the sight of Agnes, the love of my youth, when I was in Norway now."[16] His younger brother has been transformed into an accused murderer. While still feeling healthy, John nevertheless is acutely aware of his fifty years. The narrator frequently refers to the ticking of clocks,[17] and one of John's most significant acts after returning to San Francisco is to exchange his old, noisy wall clock for a new, silent one: "I have been sitting here looking at the clock in front of me. The long second hand was floating silently against its background. It is a clock without sound. Before I went to Norway an old Toten clock was standing here speaking about time passing. I had it removed when I returned home. Couldn't take the sound any more. I want solitude and silence."[18] As a result of his voyage home, John Torson no longer desires the clock to remind him of new tasks and obligations. Instead the silent clock informs him of time that merely moves

around in endless circles: "I have been sitting for a long time
looking at the wall clock, at the long second hand swinging
silently in its circle."[19]

John's new attitude towards time reflects a new attitude
towards life. No longer need he hurry on: "I have been writing on
this several evenings. Just now it is three o'clock at night, I
don't want to go to bed. While I am sitting here in great peace,
my thoughts are wandering far and wide . . . ."[20] Only once does
he mention the need to rise in the morning to carry out duties in
the factory: "I have been writing all night, and in four hours I
ought to be at the office. There are important decisions to make
every day. Business is increasing in great leaps."[21] John's
feelings towards the factory are affectionate, like those of a
father towards a child: "It is growing so fast that it is hard to
keep up, and it is a joy to behold."[22] Nevertheless, the child has
become independent of its father: "The thought struck me again, it
comes upon me every day. You better give it up now, Johannes, sell
your interest and plant cabbage."[23] In fact, John's factory-child
must share its father's affection with two new children that he
conceived in Norway. The first is the little boy he has committed
himself never to see; the second is the manuscript he is poring
over amorously during those long nights in San Francisco.

Nothing, in fact, can draw John away from his meditation and
writing. His commitment is to explain the purpose of his life by
organizing the events of the key year and a half of it and to leave
the manuscript to his unseen son in the form of a letter-testament.
It is this independence and dedication that award him the sensation
of harmony and peace. The serene mood lasts until the very last
section of the novel, when time at last catches up with John
Torson. The letter to his son is virtually finished; only the
final word is left to be written. At this point John's two servants, Carlson and Mary, enter the room and frantically start pre-
paring a trip the three are about to undertake: "Why did I agree
to leave?" John asks himself as he attempts to get the final word
down on paper: "Now Carlson is pulling out a drawer, I have to
push the chair back and write, my eyes half a meter away from the
paper."[24] John never finds the final word, as Carlson firmly pulls
him away from his writing. The servant informs him that his time
is up. The conclusion may be interpreted in several ways. Above
all, it is impossible for a human being to live a completely static
life, insulated from change. Forces beyond his control will
inevitably intrude and persuade the individual to move on. In John
Torson's case it is impossible to decide with any certainty whether
the order to leave is motivated by impending death, by the narrator's subconscious awareness that the journey must continue, or
simply by the fact that his project has concluded. There indeed is
nothing more to say.

The Immigrant

Despite his material success in America John Torson thinks of himself as an outsider. Literally speaking, he is an immigrant who left his homeland without ever setting down roots in his new country. Ross Dane and the first generation farmers in Beaver Coulee were not psychological immigrants. On the other hand there exist alienated individuals who remain immigrants all their lives, without necessarily leaving home. One such example is a figure with whom John identifies several times in the novel, the poet A. O. Vinje, in whose work such status is described with sadness.

John went to the United States not in search of a new home, but in search of wealth and success, which he would throw in the faces of those old acquaintances who had remained in Norway. Just as he was faithful to Agnes, his first love, for more than thirty years, so too he was faithful to the country of his childhood and youth. In fact, he speaks of himself as "the country's unhappy lover."[25] His great trip, then, is only in part a sentimental journey back towards a lost Agnes; it also is a voyage in search of home, one which will bring to conclusion his immigrant status and return him to the paradise from which he feels he had been expelled three decades earlier.

Seeing Agnes, of course, taught him the obvious lesson that time changes human beings. Unwilling to accept the consequences of this lesson, he discovers in Susanne a surrogate for his lost love. His reunion with Norway is different. The country has changed less than his beloved. The house where he used to live still is there, its rooms unchanged, and surrounded by the familiar garden. But the people are gone. John's father and mother are dead, and the family home now is owned by Jenny's grandfather. In a moment of despair John considers purchasing the house, but abandons the idea, presumably comprehending that it is impossible to buy back the past. John also will discover how he himself has changed. In the eyes of the Norwegians, he no longer is Johannes Torsen from Gjørstad, but rather a wealthy, middle-aged American who is paying a sentimental visit to the old country. Far from fitting into the environment, he feels rude and awkward, even more so when his hotel clerk prefers to address him in English, "because I used so many w's and addressed him with the informal pronoun 'du'."[26] John realizes that the break he had made at the age of twenty cannot be bridged: "I was thrown into a different kind of life, I had found my destiny in the promised land, where all dreams die . . . ."[27] The narrator repeatedly emphasizes that during his eighteen months in Norway he remained an outsider, observing the country and its inhabitants as through a pane of glass.

Through his writing, however, John will discover that his outsider status has been both psychological and self-imposed. In the novel the glass pane becomes a symbol of the protagonist's mental seclusion. It is a shield between himself and the outside world. In Norway as well as in America John's eternal fear of making a

commitment leaves him an outsider. A fear that Susanne may try to
tear down the glass wall causes him to shy away from marriage with
her despite his obvious love: "She would during five or ten years
have knocked her hands against a glass wall and never been able to
enter."[28] Elsewhere he states in more general terms: "If someone
attempts to penetrate the glass wall with which I surround myself,
he will be seriously hurt."[29]

The writing process itself gradually unveils John's self-
imposed exile. For more than three decades he persuaded himself
that he had left Norway because of Agnes's betrayal. However, as
he writes it becomes clear that the real reason for his departure
had not been fear of losing Agnes, but rather a fear of tying himself to her: "If I were to have Agnes, it would have been a grey
and poor Gjørstad-existence. I envisioned this future and was
frightened. Once married, a woman was faithful, with only rare
exceptions. But I saw ahead of me many years of poor pay, a hori-
zon which would become narrower every day, until it had finally
shrunk into the walls of the coffin."[30] Going to America had provided John with an escape from his passion for Agnes, an escape
from a sexual commitment he considered equivalent to a living
death. Unlike Charles Villeneuve in <u>Ross Dane</u>, whose sexuality
prevailed over his reason, John rejected sexuality because it would
channel his life into a direction which his reason refused to
accept. Moreover, after his departure, he turned Agnes into a
vision, the shield that would protect him from becoming seriously
involved with any other woman. Because a happy sexual commitment
was more than John Torson was willing to bear, he voluntarily
selected for himself the role of unhappy lover. A case in point is
the story he relates about Mary Brooke, the nightclub dancer who
remained a virgin until the evening she danced for John in her
home. The story of Mary is fragmented and veiled in mystery.
John's memory of her is associated with shadows, the white house in
which she lived, whiteness, disappearance, and death. It is
strongly suggested in the novel that John himself may have
contributed to Mary's disappearance. Once another human being came
close enough to him to threaten his solitude, she had to be
removed.

John's inclination is to flee involvement. Most poignant,
perhaps, are the narrator's fragmented memories of John's father,
who towards the end of his life became blind. In his loneliness
the old man tried to reestablish contact with his eldest son across
the ocean: "In front of me lies a letter from my father. He was
blind when he wrote it. He had never heard from me, and had the
letter delivered through the foreign ministry. A couple of the
lines he wrote crossed each other."[31] However, the son refused to
respond to the old man's cry for contact and guidance. In similar
fashion, John left Jenny at the moment when, pregnant with his
child, she needed him most. His promise to provide for both mother
and child was a poor substitute for the love he denied them.

Susanne, the woman he professes to love throughout the novel,
was abandoned as well. The narrator describes her as a woman

totally dependent on whoever happens to be her latest lover. In
order to fulfill a new love, she is ever willing to betray those
who had previously been close to her. Thus, when John Torson came
along, she abandoned not only Gunder, a man of absolute loyalty and
integrity, but also her daughter Gullan and brother-in-law Tryggve.
While admitting that it is difficult to write about Susanne, the
narrator associates her (as he did Agnes) with betrayal. Curiously, the very first line of the novel informs us that Susanne has
just perished in a German prison camp. While we never learn how
she got there, it appears obvious that her personality must have
been more complex than the narrator gives her credit for. Susanne,
the woman of betrayal, apparently had made a firm commitment to her
country and to fundamental human ideals resulting in her death.

One may contrast Susanne's fate with Torson's life following
the German invasion. Norway's "unhappy lover" by chance finds himself in Oslo on April 9, 1940. Instead of leaping into the fray to
preserve the honor of his professed beloved homeland, John never
makes a commitment to fight or resist. To be sure, as he recalls
the post-invasion months, the narrator expresses sadness and aston-
ishment. But in September 1940 he was back in San Francisco. He
passed the first year of his sojourn in Norway experiencing several
love affairs, got a woman half his age pregnant, broke up a marriage, was drunk much of the time, was mysteriously implicated in a
murder, and spent innumerable hours in a popular cafe in Oslo.
During the time following the German attack, except for deciding to
leave Norway as soon as he was able, his life did not change sub-
stantially. Just as he had left Agnes, Mary, Jenny, Susanne, and
Karl Manfred, just as he had failed his blind father, he does not
hesitate to escape from occupied Norway. In this context, it is
instructive to contrast John Torson with uncle René in Johan
Borgen's Lillelord trilogy. René's great romantic love was Paris.
Upon learning of the German occupation of the city, he resolutely
packed₂his suitcases to be with his beloved city in her most tragic
hour.[32]   Uncle René is a moving, though comical, symbol of faithfulness, John Torson represents betrayal. Writing, however,
exposes and liberates him: "I have written about those people who
used to sit at cafe Hjørnet. I am glad I have known them. They
went to prison, or they went to the wall, they will never return to
Hjørnet again, but their shadows will frequently appear between the
tables. They stood with bent heads when they had done their duty
and the day arrived. They said neither yes nor no. They went down
to the kingdom of death, and even there the apostate in vain will
ask them forgiveness."[33]   There is nothing John despises more than
betrayal; "I become nauseous when I read about faithlessness," he
writes.[34]   Or else, "I become ill when I see a movie about faithlessness, or when I read about such things in the newspapers."[35]
Yet his long, pitilessly honest self-analysis will lead him to the
sad discovery that the greatest, in fact perhaps the only genuine
traitor in the novel, is himself. Even Bjørn Lund, Jenny's playboy
father, who joins the Norwegian Nazis, will appear to have had a
crisis of consciousness, redeeming himself through suicide.

The polar opposite of John is Susanne's husband, Gunder
Gundersen. Recalling Gunder at the beginning of the novel, the
narrator emphasizes his resemblance to a faithful dog: "When I now
remember his helpless eyes, devoted and hurt like a dog's,--then I
make sure to forget the sight quickly."[36] Gunder's generosity contrasts sharply with John's egoism: "Gunder wanted to share the
world with someone. I wanted to have a world for myself."[37]
Gunder's art is closely related to his desire to investigate human
motivation. The narrator recalls meeting Gunder one night running
down an Oslo street clearly drunk: "I was yelling: Hi Gunder,
what are you chasing? The truth, the truth, he said."[38] Gunder
wishes to understand why people behave irrationally.[39] In fact, it
is the observation of suffering caused by the irrational behavior
of others that inspires Gunder to write in the first place. The
discovery of betrayal by Susanne and John, however, breaks Gunder;
irrationality gains control over his own personality and he begins
to resemble his insane twin brother, Tryggve.

Once settled in his house in San Francisco, it is John who
will continue Gunder's quest for the truth about people. The narrator recognizes that Gunder's hand guides him as he writes.
Reviewing all his betrayals, it is perhaps that of Gunder which
most torments the narrator. By continuing Gunder's work, he is
able to redeem his guilt and turn betrayal into an act of
creativity.

The Murder Mystery

On one level The Past Is a Dream is a mystery novel, in which
the protagonist/narrator tries to discover who murdered Anton
Strand. John Torson travels to the site of the murder, interviews
appropriate individuals, takes a trip to Anton's hometown, talks to
the dead man's father, and visits the cemetery where the victim is
buried. As the narrator reviews and reorganizes his notes, the
evidence incriminates John himself. It is likely that a dazed
John, carrying a loaded pistol, entered the garden at Gjørstad
during the evening of the murder. He had come to Gjørstad to use
the weapon somehow, perhaps to take revenge upon a society that in
his view had deprived him of country, home, and love: "There was
no motive to shoot a particular person, only a motive to shoot."[40]
On seeing another man in the garden, also with a gun in hand, John
instinctively aimed his weapon at the intruder and pulled the
trigger. Somehow, during the remainder of his stay in Norway, John
would manage to block the incident out of his mind. During the
process of writing about the events in the old country, however,
fragmented descriptions would surface--of the garden, of the
corpse, of looking through a window and seeing Jenny with a long
glass tube bent over a man in an easy chair. While each of these
descriptions might be explained as a figment of John's vivid
imagination, his intimate knowledge of the house and garden, and
his attentive presence at the trial of Karl Manfred, the narrator
insists upon using the fragments as pieces of a puzzle to be used

against John himself. In similar fashion the narrator will impli-
cate John in the disappearance of Mary Brooke, and the drowning of
Røde Hendrik, his successor as Agnes's lover three decades earlier.
Whether or not John is actually guilty of murder is impossible to
prove. John may in fact be compared to the millionaire in a story
to which the narrator refers several times in the course of the
novel: "There was a man in Los Angeles who embezzled and falsified
his business records for many years. In the end he could not take
it any longer, and gave himself up. He remained in prison a year,
while they finished scrutinizing his books. The papers were full
of stories about his daring swindles.

"Not a cent was missing. He had fabricated it all in order to
cover something he had never done."[41]   The Los Angeles executive
had such an overwhelming feeling of psychological guilt that he
constructed a self-incriminating criminal case. Redemption arrived
through punishment. John may have had similar motives. During the
long evenings spent reading his notes, contemplating his past,
organizing and writing, the narrator obtains a sort of redemption
through self-reflection. Consequently the external events of the
murder mystery become less significant: "When I read through what
I had written in order to find proof against myself for the murder
of Anton Strand, I included as well some of the things I have men-
tioned about Mary Brooke. But of course it was nothing more than a
game."[42]

Whether or not John actually killed Anton Strand is less
important than most critics of the novel have believed. Spatially
the murder mystery occupies a relatively minor place in The Past Is
a Dream. Far more important is John Torson's discovery of his true
self, that of a traitor, and his subsequent transformation into an
artist. The commitment John was unable to establish either towards
others or towards Norway, he makes spontaneously in his writing.

The Face in the Mirror

While organizing his diary, John Torson will gradually discover his identity. The self-image of a relatively youthful,
wealthy fifty-year-old Norwegian-American who returned to his homeland to recapture a woman who had mistreated him a generation
earlier is profoundly jolted. The transformation that takes place
can be compared to the physical transformation of John during a
bombing attack at the docks of Oslo: "When I was able to think
again I stood raving not far from the crates which had been torn
into shreds. I was chewing and spitting. I had earth in my mouth
and dust in my eyes. Something was wrong with my hearing, I
couldn't hear a sound for a long while. Bombs were falling less
than fifty meters away from me, on the mountain up towards the fortress. A gate was torn apart and a couple of leafy trees were
slashed.

"I had been lying in the street. A short distance away among earth and sharp stones were my cigarette and my hat. The cigarette was torn open. Knocked out of my mouth by a small stone. Heaven had punished a gentleman who was standing there smoking a cigar. I myself was whole, but quite muddy."[43] The narrator clearly paints John as a survivor, one who managed to go through a very serious crisis without being destroyed by it,--"whole, but quite muddy." In the course of the novel John is frequently described in front of a mirror which often reflects an unrecognizable face. He has his first mirror experience very early in the novel. Walking through the streets of Oslo, he suddenly stopped and peered into a store window. A strange face stared back at him: "A face that was mine, a death mask with living eyes. Unshaved and with a dirty collar. A part of the person I saw in that mirror was going to pursue me."[44] The face in the mirror is, of course, an unsavory part of John himself.

Often other people serve as John's mirrors. Looking at gardener Lund, a relative of Jenny's, he discovers in the other's face traits that he recognizes as his own: "I felt ill at ease when I saw gardener Lund, I remembered a photograph of myself at that age, and it wasn't funny. We didn't look alike, but there was something in the eyes, the youthful, sluggish stare. I sense that a part of my youth was sitting in front of me, and I didn't want it back."[45] Looking at his brother Karl Manfred: "He was skinnier than I, and taller. We looked alike. There was something brutal by the mouth that I didn't recognize from my own face."[46] John does know that the face he perceives in his various mirrors belongs to a dark, suppressed self, his shadow or double. Gunder once says to him: "Can you imagine anything more banal than a person without a double? He cannot confront himself, and he doesn't hear his own unhappy cry."[47] What John Torson glimpses in the mirror is the irrational, perverse side of himself. Poe's words, "Perverseness is one of the primitive impulses of the human heart,"[48] frequently runs through the narrator's mind. On two separate occasions he cites the following stanza by Asmund Olafson Vinje:

> Um du for den rette spegelen stod,
> og såg so ditt sanne verd,
> du da måtte tape ditt livsens mod,
> for det du slik stakkar er.[49]

The reflected side of the personality, whether seen in a mirror or in the face of another individual, is absolutely essential if one is to perceive the complete self. This dark shadow is evasive, as it tends to sink back into the darkness of the subconscious almost as soon as it has appeared on the surface: "I had wanted to show me to myself, but I had disappeared unseen before I saw me."[50] What Sandemose means is that every Dr. Jekyll has a Mr. Hyde hidden within. One may consider The Past Is a Dream as a novel about John Torson's discovery of his double and of confrontation with his dark shadow. Thus the narrator persistently underscores the unsavory side of the protagonist's personality.

The outcome of the investigation is painful. Facing his brother, who after his trial, prison term, and loss of Jenny, is a broken man, John perceives himself: "not a good, not even a decent human being. Perhaps I had been one, or could have become one, if I had escaped my youth intact. A difficult adolescence seldom results in good people, but people who are easily hurt, vengeful, difficult, hermits, or Hitler types."[51]

The narrator observes in Hitler and the Germans traits that he recognizes in himself--tyrannical, aggressive tendencies, perversities. At the root of the problem is an inability to establish contact with other people: "The German suffers from an inability to establish contact with others, and he attributes the fault to them. So he shoots, and as 'grosser Wohltäter und Befreier der Kulturwelt' he tramples on our world and kills those who are not embracing him."[52] In a similar manner, after thirty years' absence, John Torson had invaded Norway armed with his dollars, bravado, and heavy American accent. Like the Germans, John deluded himself into considering himself a benefactor, paying for dinners, drinks, and friendships, and quite readily lending money to those who needed it. The victims put up virtually no resistance. Jenny, Susanne, even Gunder capitulated without putting up a fight. In fact, unlike the victims of the Germans, those of John are precisely the ones who would embrace him as friend or lover. Like the Germans, however, John thinks of himself as a victor, never dreaming that a day of reckoning will ever come: "Let it never be forgotten that the German showed us his true face, when he believed he was going to win this war, when he thought that the day of reckoning would never come."[53] The narrator understands how John played with the lives of others, leaving chaos, disruption, and even death in his path, never expecting to be held accountable for his deeds. Like the German invasion of April 9, 1940, John's arrival in Norway provoked a moral crisis, a virtual collective psychological collapse: "We saw people being killed, values destroyed, we felt how the ties between people who loved each other were torn apart. What we sensed was the defeat of humanity, not that of Norway . . . ."[54] Yet the victimization turns out to be temporary: "The Germans, then, had achieved what they wanted, they had made us lame. But they had grossly underestimated what can root itself and grow in the individual who has been struck to the ground."[55]

In the long run the humane instincts will prevail over the inhumane ones. In a moral struggle humanity will only permit itself to sink to a certain point: "This far but no further."[56] The struggle to regain dignity, however, will be long and hard, and it will take the form of battling against the evil both within one's self and outside it: "One knew that before this was restored, one would have to live many years, and fight, fight against the stupidity and evil in oneself and others."[57] In a peculiarly negative way the characters in The Past Is a Dream appear to win the war against the evil within themselves. Susanne pays with her life in a German concentration camp, Jenny breaks off communication with

her adored father. Bjørn Lund redeems himself by taking his own
life. Yet, on the personal level, in their struggle against John,
they all seem to be losers. John himself, however, ultimately has
to face his day of judgment through his own writing. According to
Ibsen, the act of writing is precisely to stage a tribunal against
oneself.[58] It will take John four years to redeem his guilt. The
period of time, moreover, seems much longer, since it transforms
the youthful fifty-year old John Torson into "an old man in his
servant's power."[59] Nevertheless, the experience turns out to be a
positive and even pleasurable one. In this respect John Torson
resembles Belacqua, a slothful figure in the <u>Divine Comedy</u>, whom
Dante observes on the slopes of Purgatory condemned to spend a
number of years equivalent to his lifetime contemplating his past.
For the Florentine, however, such "punishment" turns out to be a
blessing in disguise, because he can conceive of no greater pleasure than to meditate upon a life of torpor.[60] For his part, John
Torson in the end resents being pulled away from his desk and his
papers by his servant, Carlson, who informs John that his time is
up and that he must now move on.

John Torson is both destroyer and builder welded into a single
character. He insinuates himself into relationships and families,
destroying the couple Jenny--Karl Manfred as well as the quartet
Susanne-Gunder-Gullan-Tryggve. Wherever he enters, he brings
rupture in his wake. Yet, in a negative sense, John is a builder
of his tool factory, of his large, comfortable house in San
Francisco. John's constructions are intended to be protective
walls sheltering him from other people. The money made on his factory enabled him to gain independence of others and in fact render
them dependent upon him. The house in San Francisco was as protected as a <u>chateau-fort</u>. In <u>The Tar Dealer</u> the protagonist, Audun
Hamre, has his house/fortress invaded by pitiless outsiders, and is
driven to the desperate solution of lighting an already installed
fuse, destroying himself and the intruders alike. John Torson is
more fortunate. He is the builder of a novel, a work of art, and
in his writing he discovers a safety valve which permits <u>him</u> to become a survivor. The dishonesty of his life is redeemed through
the honesty of his art. His writing not only helps John discover
who he genuinely is, but it also enables him to communicate with
others in a non-threatening way. Characteristically enough, he
insists throughout the book that the son will only be permitted to
read the manuscript after his father's death, that is after John's
privacy can no longer be challenged.

Notes

1. *Verker i utvalg*, V, p. 237.

2. *Ibid.* Sandemose's italics.

3. *Ibid.*, p. 234.

4. Asmund Lien, "Store John vender tilbake." *Edda*, no. 65 (1965), p. 342.

5. *Verker i utvalg*, V, p. 283.

6. *Ibid.*, p. 39.

7. Lien, "Store John vender tilbake," pp. 368-69.

8. *Ibid.*, p. 382.

9. *Verker i utvalg*, V, p. 115.

10. *Ibid.*, p. 282.

11. *Ibid.*, p. 9.

12. *Ibid.*, p. 7.

13. *Ibid.*, p. 195.

14. Hans Meyerhoff, *Time in Literature*. Berkeley and Los Angeles: University of California Press, 1960, pp. 5, 31.

15. *Verker i utvalg*, V, p. 195.

16. *Ibid.*, p. 28.

17. *Ibid.*, pp. 131, 208.

18. *Ibid.*, p. 40.

19. *Ibid.*, p. 67.

20. *Ibid.*, p. 40.

21. *Ibid.*, p. 45.

22. *Ibid.*

23. *Ibid.*

24. *Ibid.*, p. 283.

25. Ibid., p. 98.

26. Ibid., p. 47.

27. Ibid., p. 104.

28. Ibid., p. 135.

29. Ibid., p. 201.

30. Ibid., p. 33.

31. Ibid., p. 154.

32. Johan Borgen, De mørke kilder. Oslo: Gyldendal, 1956, p. 136.

33. Verker i utvalg, V, p. 9.

34. Ibid., p. 65.

35. Ibid., p. 76.

36. Ibid., p. 14.

37. Ibid., p. 136.

38. Ibid., p. 252.

39. Ibid., p. 221, 223.

40. Ibid., p. 108.

41. Ibid., pp. 73-74.

42. Ibid., p. 267.

43. Ibid., p. 17.

44. Ibid., p. 16.

45. Ibid., pp. 205-06.

46. Ibid., pp. 207-08.

47. Ibid., pp. 220.

48. Ibid., p. 163. Sandemose's italics.

49. Ibid., pp. 163, 181. Vinje's poem can be roughly translated in the following way:

"If you were standing by the right mirror,
and thus saw your true worth,
then you would lose your courage to live
because you are such a miserable wreck."

50. Verker i utvalg, V, p. 194.

51. Ibid., p. 209.

52. Ibid., p. 105.

53. Ibid., p. 192.

54. Ibid., p. 236.

55. Ibid., p. 237.

56. Ibid., p. 241.

57. Ibid., p. 237.

58. "Å leve --er krig med trolle/ i hjertets og hjernens hvelv. Å
dikte, -- det er å holde/ dommedag over seg selv."

59. Verker i utvalg, V, p. 282.

60. Belacqua is described in the fourth Canto of Dante's
Purgatorio.

8.

Alice Atkinson and Her Lovers:
Solitude and Artistic Sublimation

Chronologically, Alice Atkinson and Her Lovers continues where
The Past Is a Dream left off. The novel focuses on Europe during
and immediately after World War II. Like The Past Is a Dream and A
Fugitive Crosses His Tracks it is a kind of epistolary novel, the
revised version of a series of letters from Jørgen Haukli to his
sister. The first and by far the longest section, 125 of the
novel's 138 pages, is dated Oslo, Summer '45, and is an amalgam of
several letters. It is written from a shabby hotel room where
Haukli has been lodging since his return from England after the end
of the war. The second letter (eleven pages) is dated Bristol,
February '45. The third letter (only two pages) is again written
from the hotel room in Oslo and dated Autumn '45. Spatially, the
novel can be seen as a long main section followed by two epilogues.

The Plot

In section I, the narrator tells three seemingly different,
but nevertheless interrelated, stories. The first one deals with
Haukli's experience of spending thirty-three days alone on a high
mountain shelf in Germany where his parachute had landed after the
plane he was flying was hit by gun fire. On the shelf he discovered the skeleton of a stone age man whom he calls Større, "the
greater one." Haukli managed to escape from the shelf, somehow
succeeded in making his way out of Germany, and ultimately wound up
as a member of British Intelligence. The second story deals with
Haukli's work in Bristol, his strange relationship to the other
three members of the unit, Alexander Selkirk, William Lee, and
Alice Atkinson, with whom he shared a house. Haukli fell deeply in

love with Alice, who, on her side showed no interest in him, apparently preferring both Selkirk and Lee. Selkirk, in fact, was the leader of the ring and Alice frequently spent the night in his room. The two also regularly made trips together. Ultimately, Selkirk and Alice both disappeared, and Lee, who was jealous of Selkirk, was accused of murder, tried, and sentenced to death by hanging. While Haukli had good reason to believe that Selkirk was still alive, he refrained from involving himself in the case. The third story describes Haukli's friendship with Torgrim, a fellow Norwegian he met in England. Wounded in a leg, Torgrim served the cause of the Allies by cutting out articles about the war from newspapers and magazines. All his thoughts, however, were dedicated to his wife and young daughter he had left in Norway. Torgrim was dreaming of returning home loaded with the gifts he had accumulated during his years abroad. Liberation finally came and Torgrim immediately set out to realize his dream, only to discover that his wife had both a new man and a new child, and that he himself was no longer wanted. After a period of grief and keen disappointment Torgrim rallied, remarried, and appeared ready to start a new life.

The three stories in the main section of Alice Atkinson are related in such a way that the story of Torgrim and that of Større and the mountain shelf provide a framework for the central one dealing with Alice Atkinson and the Bristol intelligence network. Torgrim and Større come to represent two contrasting solutions to Haukli's own problem, either a reentry into the world, through marriage and family, or a complete withdrawal into the self, with no human contacts other than his mental creations, the figments of his own imagination. Ultimately Haukli will reject both solutions, in favor of a practical, detached relationship to others supplemented by a more profound kind of communication through art.

The second letter, or first epilogue, was written during the hours following the execution of William Lee. In his imagination Haukli was living through Lee's final night in the prison cell. The letter reveals an extraordinarily guilty conscience. The third and final letter of the novel reveals that Alice herself had been found dead in a hotel room in London in March, long before Haukli had left England. The death was considered to be suicide. Because of Haukli's guilty conscience and the chronology of the events, some critics believe that Haukli himself had visited Alice in the hotel room, killed[1] her, and then suppressed the whole incident from his consciousness. The evidence to back up such a reading appears thin. On the other hand, it would provide a parallel to the standard reading of The Past Is a Dream, where John Torson, cast in the double role of detective and criminal, was systematically building up a case against himself.

Alice Atkinson and Her Lovers is a pessimistic and difficult novel, dealing with disillusionment, misunderstanding, unrequited love, guilt, and the near impossibility of understanding chains of events completely. The weakness of the book is that too much of the material which would have been necessary in order to understand fully the action and the characters is suppressed. Some of this material was presumably included in the letters Haukli had originally written to his sister, but which he decided not to send: "I have promised you the letters, and they were written to you. But when I read them through once again two weeks ago, I understood that I would never part with them, and now they no longer exist. Instead they have been used as a basis for what I have written to you. There were things in those letters that I am happy nobody will ever see, since those letters were written during a period when I was often unhappy."[2] Presumably Haukli destroyed the original letters because he was afraid that they would reveal more about himself than he wanted to share, even with his beloved sister. However, because of the suppression of presumably essential material, it is difficult to arrive at a coherent interpretation of <u>Alice Atkinson</u>. Haukli's letters are fragmented, and the reader frequently feels like one of the zoologists the narrator mentions, "who reconstruct a prehistoric animal on the basis of a few bone fragments."[3] Haukli himself, of course, undertakes a similar reconstruction when he attempts to put together the story of Større on the basis of the remnants of a centuries-old skeleton which he runs across on the mountain shelf.

On the other hand, the many blanks in the fiction, stories that appear contradictory or incomplete, characters that we are unable to know, a narrator who is reluctant or unable to express his thoughts and feelings, are what give the novel its special tone as well as its distinctly modernistic stamp. Is Sandemose, like his French fellow novelists Alain Robbe-Grillet and Claude Simon, telling us that reconstruction of the past is indeed impossible, and that the modern novel must precisely reflect and comment upon this impossibility?

Despair and the Genesis of Writing

Sitting in his shabby hotel room in Oslo after the end of the war, Jørgen Haukli feels miserable. Moreover, his sensation of loneliness is intense, he has no access to other people, and he sees no future for either himself or for post-war Norway: "Sister, I am sitting here in a sad hotel room in Oslo feeling miserable. The thought that life is not worth living is very close to the surface. And it is not only I who feel that way. How sad Oslo has become after the war!"[4] His depressed state evokes in him a nostalgia for childhood, especially the happiness and security he had felt in the company of his younger sister. The sister incarnated for Haukli warmth and love, and it is not surprising that he will cope with his present misery by attempting to reestablish a line of communication with her through his letters. In fact, as he writes he senses her actual presence in the room, relieving him from his terrifying loneliness: "--for I have felt that way several times while I was writing: You were here in the room, and I was talking. I have felt pretty good while writing, and amazingly often I have been sitting here thinking of how we played as children, you and I. When I have heard or read about family disputes, I have always felt happy remembering what good friends you and I have been."[5] The need to "talk" to his sister started in England, where Haukli felt as if he were suffocating in a labyrinth of silence and secrecy: "Still, I had to have air, and so I started the letters to you."[6] Haukli's mood as he writes is very different, indeed, from that of John Torson, who was enjoying his long, lonely nights of contemplation in the comfort of his San Francisco home. Haukli, on the other hand, is uncomfortable, and is writing half automatically, hoping that somehow the writing will lead him onto a track which will enable him to escape from the mental labyrinth where he is trapped: "Yes, I am circling around this point, finding no road, and writing half automatically in the hope that I may find a track, a stable point. I am, you see, suffering because of this. Something is bothering me."[7] The writing does help Haukli, in the sense that it relieves the pressure of secrecy, making it progressively easier for him to express things which he had earlier either kept inside or blotted out of his mind altogether: "As I write I can feel how the pressure disappears. It is no longer important to keep quiet."[8]

While Haukli started to write as an act of desperation, the process will gradually generate a new and more ambitious goal, namely to enable a complete and unobstructed vision of his own self: "In a moment of concentration I was to meet myself."[9] Miraculously, this meeting with the self will lift Haukli out of his humdrum daily existence and provide him with the key to all enigmas: "I would be able to walk without getting tired, float in the air without anybody noticing it. Move from place to place just by wishing to do so. Turn the pages of the book of life and read a simple, earthshaking truth. Travel into space and see the moon from the other side. Enter another level. Or only see myself in a split second and then know all. For I knew that no one has seen himself, and the one who has solved his own enigma has turned everything else into trivia and busy work."[10] While the miracle never does occur, the narrator expresses contentment that this should be so: "I am as a matter of fact happy that it hasn't happened yet. Many pleasures that I have had, might then become small or disappear. Why should the all-knowing read books?"[11] The narrator realizes that just as an erotic fantasy will die once it is lived out in real life, so is his dream of a miracle most fascinating while it is still a dream: "When this miracle has happened, I do not know what to do."[12]

Oslo 1945

Haukli's despair at the beginning of Alice Atkinson can be explained as the letdown that succeeds intense anticipation. After several years of exile and war, he is finally returning home to a country at peace. Instead he finds himself in a seemingly dead city, where no one stretches out a hand to welcome him back: "So I

stood at Fornebu [airport], and I wish to tell you that I could
have cried. Now I knew that something had fallen apart, and that I
had returned home in order to force Norway to become my country
once again. Subsequently I walked down Karl Johan Street and felt
as if I had landed on the moon, I who had lived in this city for
ten years, attended the University here and been happy. On top of
it all, the first thing I learned was that you were still ill in
Sweden. I tried to call some old acquaintances. No one knew where
they were. Whether they were in Norway? No, they didn't know. A
distance had appeared between people. Then I entered the hotel and
sat looking out the window. Suddenly I wanted a drink.

"It didn't exist."[13]

A general greyness pervades the atmosphere, and life keeps
moving around in circles as routinely as an old alarm clock.[14]
Haukli, of course, does not possess John Torson's serene outlook
upon the passage of time. At the end of the novel Haukli's
environment has not really changed. Looking up from his sheets of
paper, he suddenly has the sensation of Alice Atkinson's eyes
staring at him, and spontaneously he asks her what the future has
in store. Alice's answer takes the form of a vision: "I saw that
there was no future. Yes, time existed, but it had disconnected
us. I arrived in Oslo in the midst of this future . . . There were
no people to be seen. I was the only living being in the whole
city. The roofs had caved in, and the houses showed gaping signs
of degeneration. There were no signs of people or any kinds of
animals. Only in the overgrown Studenterlunden I saw some bone
remnants of pigeons and sparrows. It almost killed me that there
wasn't even a skeleton to be seen, and this city at the verge of
collapse had not been bombed. It was just withering away because
it had lost its soul, its people."[15] Moreover, the all-pervasive
atmosphere of death is not limited to Oslo alone: "There was no
life in Norway. So I wanted to see cities in Europe, I was in
Stockholm, Copenhagen, Leningrad, Moscow, Berlin, Paris, and
London. Then I couldn't take it any more. There was no life in
Europe, but in the Seine and the Thames I had seen mounds of skele-
tons."[16]

Haukli's writing does not transform his vision of post-war
Europe as a continent which had lost its soul, but it does change
his own attitude towards the situation and his ability to cope with
it. If genuine peace never arrives on an external level, the
writing unexpectedly helps Haukli attain the inner peace which he
had formerly been lacking: "Right now I care about nothing but
peace and solitude,"[17] he explains. He considers and then rejects
the possibility of returning to the mountain shelf in Germany in
favor of the more practical solution of going to the mountains with
his friends, Torgrim and Tora. Haukli has opted for an escape
which is well within reach. The unattainable Alice Atkinson, whore
and madonna welded into one, has been replaced by Torgrim's new
wife, Tora, reduced to the traditional role of domestic servant:
"Tora will come along to cook."

On the Mountain Shelf

The thirty-three days Haukli spent on the mountain shelf provided him with an extreme experience of solitude. He had sufficient provisions to keep him alive and relatively comfortable for
several weeks. After having inspected his immediate surroundings
he decided that there was no apparent possibility of escaping.
Only distant noises from planes and bombs broke the deadly silence
and reminded him that the outside world still existed. Haukli's
exile on the shelf became an existential experience of the human
condition. He knew that certain death awaited him once his provisions ran out, since no life-sustaining vegetation grew on the
bare shelf, and the steep mountain sides appeared to rule out any
possibility of escape. The awareness of death made him sense that
nothing is distinctive and nothing is important. He compared his
unlikely landing to that of an autumn leaf falling from the sky,
and mused over the nourishment his own body would ultimately provide to the sparse vegetation around him.[18]   That the planes occasionally circling above his head could be means of rescue never
entered his mind. On the contrary, when hearing the noise above he
instinctively sought shelter in the bushes. While Haukli did not
consciously want to die, the instinctive fear of the evil he associated with other people was greater than his fear of death.

During his inspection of the shelf, Haukli discovered the
mouth of a cave which had been covered with rocks. A breath of air
within the cave made him presume that there must be an opening on
the other side. Haukli started a laborious climb through the cave,
but his progression was abruptly halted by a chorus of piercing
screams which chilled him to the bone. Quite naturally he had the
sensation of having reached the gate of hell: "I am standing at
the gate of hell, and the demons were welcoming me with screams."[19]
He turned around and headed back to the original shelf, which he
now associated with "home," "nest," and safety.

The horrible screams nevertheless stimulated Haukli to reeval-
uate his own situation. His most dangerous enemy proved not to be
human after all: "I had heard the enemy sound and had him in front
of me, with an ocean of fog behind, and alone. The enemy was no
human, perhaps the sterile war god himself, who doesn't hear your
anguished cries any more than you hear the bread pleading for
itself in your mouth."[20]   He also realized that only by uniting
would people have any hope of putting up a defense against those
forces of destruction, whether external or self-inflicted: "The
net of prejudice against which people are afraid to fight and
therefore have given the name Destiny in order to signify something
that cannot be changed. We will never experience anything but
restlessness and anguish, and one by one we will be caught."[21]   The
thought of escaping the shelf then took on a renewed sense of
urgency. The next day Haukli ventured back into the cave to
explore the mystery and possibility of finding an exit. He finally
reached his goal, only to discover that the exit was blocked by a
wall of skimpy trees that he must laboriously cut down with his

knife in order to get out on the other side. The screams started
again, and this time he realized that they came from a pair of
royal eagles in the process of feeding their young. Moreover, he
discovered that the exit from the cave would lead him onto a rock
even smaller than the one he had left behind: "There is no highway
leading to an eagle's nest,"[22] he stated philosophically. Faced
with the new situation, Haukli experienced happy excitement. The
certainty of death at the end of a fixed and limited period of time
merely added to the contentment of the moment. Haukli made a fire
from the wood he had cut down, cooked himself a cup of coffee, and
let his thoughts wander. The experience in the cave, almost
totally cut off from reality, provided him with an ideal, illuminated moment that he would always long to relive. The scene was
most likely inspired by Plato's idea that the only true life is in
the mind. In an intensely introspective mood, Haukli had the
sensation of knowing who he was: "I had time to look into myself,
and for a short while I was who I was. Closer I really didn't get
to the matter: I sat there and was who I was."[23]

After a peaceful sleep Haukli proceeded to cut through the
barrier of trees and crawl onto the rock. To his great surprise he
discovered a human skeleton with a stone axe next to it. He
figured that the skeleton must have belonged to a man who had lived
thousands of years ago. Haukli immediately thought of the skeleton
as a friend and ancestor, someone who had suffered the fate which
faced Haukli himself. He started speaking to the skeleton, answer
imaginary questions, and receive advice. He even gave the skeleton
a name, "Større," "the greater one," which shows his admiration for
his long-dead companion. He called himself Noah, saved from the
flood. Even though Haukli looked upon himself as a survivor, he
nevertheless considered the destiny of Større, who had perished in
total isolation, to be of greater significance. While strongly
attracted to Større, as Haukli's supply of food and matches started
to run out, he decided to make a desperate attempt to escape the
fate of the skeleton, to avoid death just as Noah had done. He
made a rope out of his parachute and succeeded in escaping from the
rock. Ultimately he found his way to England and became a member
of the Intelligence network. The descent from the mountain is seen
in an ambivalent way throughout the novel, a "fall" of sorts. On
the rock, with Større and the eagles as his only companions, Haukli
lived in a state of innocence, peace, and serenity. Well aware of
approaching death, the future had completely lost its meaning for
him. The company of Større gave him a feeling of solidarity across
temporal barriers. He accepted the fact that solitude and death
alone provide true peace. The description of Haukli on his rock by
the eagles' nest is reminiscent of the Prometheus myth. During the
final days of his stay, Haukli succeeded in stealing food from the
eagles, knowing that in the end the birds would have their revenge,
and nourish themselves upon his body.

The Intelligence Network

England during World War II provided Haukli with an environment in sharp contrast to the one on the mountain top. The narrator himself thinks of his stay in Bristol as an entrapment in a
labyrinth. Secrecy, false identities, mysterious disappearances,
and cryptic missions were the order of the day. In the letters he
was writing to his sister Haukli had to suppress all information
that might in any way be related to his Intelligence activities.
Above all, Haukli was expected to do his job without ever questioning its purpose or trying to put the pieces together into an
intelligible whole: "I do not like to struggle night and day with
a job whose total significance I did not understand . . . ."[24] The
experience, reminiscent of that of Joseph K in Kafka's The Trial,
made him lose completely any sense of identity. He felt like an
automaton, mechanically responding to external stimuli according to
a process calculated in advance by unknown powers: "I do not even
understand completely what I myself was. I often had the sensation
of being an almost invisible screw in the depth of an adding
machine, without personal consciousness, but sensitive to certain
stimuli to which I had been taught to be sensitive,--and then automatically transplant the impression exactly the way that too had
been learned, and not differently."[25] He was told never to ask
questions, never to investigate any incident that he might happen
to witness, however bizarre it appeared to be. Moreover, within
the quartet (Selkirk, Lee, Alice, and Haukli), Haukli was clearly
the person with least power. "A sailor on shore leave," he called
himself.

Alexander Selkirk was the chief, an inscrutable, dangerous
man, who appeared to survive all major international crises.
Haukli thought he had seen him in Oslo in April 1940 dressed in a
German uniform, and again in 1945 as a member of a group of
defeated German soldiers ready to return home. Haukli suspected
him of being a double agent. He lived upon the misery of war,
ready to stir up conflict and quench any hope for peace. Selkirk
was a "werewolf," an individual who, out of bitterness and spite
against others, had decided to curse the world: "I had a feeling
of contact with the sensitive animal Selkirk, as I have always felt
closer to lonely wolves than to those traveling in flocks."[26]
Haukli instinctively felt a kind of love/hate for Selkirk, whose
schizophrenic personality was revealed in the fascination he dis-
played for Haukli's experience on the mountain shelf. In fact,
Selkirk himself had grown up in a lighthouse, totally isolated from
society. His only human contact had been his taciturn father, and
the only language he knew well was that of the seabirds. In Alice
Atkinson Selkirk is a demonic character, at war with the world and
obsessed with the dream of returning to the solitary peace of his
childhood. He is clearly related to Jørgen Haukli himself.

While Haukli felt a certain affinity for Selkirk, he had a
distinct dislike for William Lee, the owner of the house where the
four members of the Intelligence network lived. Lee was a cat-like

character, hiding his sharp claws behind a facade of friendliness:
"In daily life I liked William Lee least, and after the initial
good impression, it didn't take long before I detested him sin-
cerely. I was bothered by his friendliness, because it had pur-
poseless claws."[27] Haukli's dislike of Lee was, of course, related
to his suspicion that Alice liked the Englishman and that she might
be unfaithful to Selkirk. A very complicated chain of events
reveals that Lee was planning to murder his rival in order to have
Alice to himself. While the plan failed and Selkirk escaped, Lee
was nevertheless hanged for a murder he presumably never committed.

Alice Atkinson, of whom we merely see scattered glimpses
through Haukli's eyes, is the central character in the novel.
Alice incarnates the distorted, ambivalent image that Sandemose's
protagonists frequently have of women. She is in the narrator's
view a disobedient Eve, a refound mother, an angel, a sister, and a
whore.[28] Hareide Aarbakke comments on this aspect of the author's
work,[29] which undoubtedly has its origin in an oedipal conflict in
the childhood home.

The most characteristic feature of the story of Alice and
Haukli is that she is completely unresponsive to his advances,
while apparently having relationships with both Selkirk and Lee in
turn. Alice existed almost exclusively in Haukli's dream world, a
Romantic love fantasy that never lost its grip because it was never
fulfilled. Haukli explains this to his sister: "You are a woman,
and you may have noticed how little I have written about Alice.
But she has been there all along. She was present when I was
telling one daydream after the other about returning home to places
where there was solitude and eternity. You see, this was something
that happened to me late, so late that I had had all too many women
described to me through eyes blinded by love not to be careful with
what I say. I unhappily know that what one loves is a construction, a dream from which you only wake up at the divorce. I presume that is when you discover who the beloved was. She was someone else. What you loved had the same value as a dream. It only
existed in your own mind, and she did not measure up to your lofty
constructions. This does not turn love into a lesser or poorer
reality, but the person in love does not speak about another individual, he is speaking about the flowers he is picking in his own
bewitched garden."[30]

Since the dream of Alice was a dream of happiness in a total,
lasting union, it is understandable that during his moments of deep
solitude Haukli felt closest to her. In fact, in the whole novel
Alice genuinely intervened only twice in Haukli's life. The first
time he saw her was at the beginning of his stay in Bristol, during
a visit she made to the hospital where Haukli was recovering after
having been struck by a car. Alice served as an intermediary
between Haukli and Selkirk, informing Haukli both of the housing
arrangements which had been made for him and of the role Selkirk
had chosen for him. It was during the hospital visit that Haukli
fell in love with Alice and she became a permanent part of his

fantasy world. The other incident involved a bicycle trip which
the two took in Bristol. The description is exceedingly brief:
"On her bicycle she came around the bend of the steep hill and flew
down towards me. She looked up towards the windows in the street
while rushing along with her dress flowing."[31]   The vision of Alice
on her bicycle was to become an "illuminated moment" for Haukli, a
flash of brightness that made his life worth living: "It is so
that the small things I experienced alone with Alice are as alive
for me as my finest childhood memories."[32]   Alice here is associated with youth, light, speed, harmony, and childhood innocence.
She is the reincarnation of the sister he used to love as a small
child. Haukli compared her to an angel flying down the dark
street, an image in sharp contrast to the one he has of her in
"clattering slippers walking in the direction of Alexander
Selkirk's room."[33]   The second image is associated with darkness,
secrecy, and sexuality, a side of life with which Sandemose's protagonists find it particularly difficult to cope. Haukli is no
exception to this rule. The following episode illustrates his
emotions in this regard.

Female Sexuality

In myth women tend frequently to be seen either as the Virgin
Mary or as Cybele, the Greek sex goddess. The "good" woman is
"pure," placed on a pedestal to be worshipped and adored. Once she
permits herself to be pulled down from this elevated position, she
is "fallen," an object of shame and disgrace. In Alice Atkinson,
as in most of Sandemose's works, women are seen in precisely this
way. A notable exception is, of course, Vera in September. The
descriptions of female sexuality are most explicit in the stories
Haukli tells about Moen's orchard, a place clearly related to
Adamsen's barn in A Fugitive Crosses His Tracks. Moen's orchard is
a place associated with transgression, since it was the favorite
spot for Jørgen and his companions to steal apples during their
childhood. The orchard is, as in previous Sandemose works, a version of the garden of Eden, with its tree of knowledge, the eating
of the forbidden fruit, and the subsequent expulsion and fall: "We
are small children who have wandered into a black catacomb with
threatening eyes scattered on the walls. In Moen's orchard stood
the tree of knowledge."[34]   Once Haukli and two of his friends had
ventured into the orchard they suddenly perceived the face of a
woman through the leaves of the trees: "Through a fence about ten
meters from us there was a face in the greenery."[35]   The face gave
the boys a chilling sensation of confronting death, and they ran
from the orchard as rapidly as they could, never to return: "How
much boys themselves believe of such things is of course hard to
tell afterwards, but already long ago we had associated all fear
with Moen's orchard."[36]

A few months later Jørgen saw the woman again, this time
seated on a bench not far from the orchard. She stood up, her
tongue hanging out of her mouth, and stretched out her arms to

embrace him: "This is how children felt when they were sacrificed
to their divinity. In a moment she would bite into my throat."[37]
The woman is here seen as a vampire who is reaching out to grab her
male victim and suck out his vitality. The boy managed to ward off
the woman's advances. Suddenly she turned around and pretended to
depart, only to lift her long skirt above her head and dance
obscenely: "I had never seen a woman the way she now was dancing.
I had fantasized about it, but not about those long, laced boots,
rough woolen stockings, and other barbaric pieces of clothing."[38]

     Ten years later Jørgen passed the orchard in the company of
his father, and the woman appeared for the third time. Jørgen
again wished to flee, but the father forced him to pay attention to
the woman. The father explained that years ago, when the woman was
a young girl, she and a group of boys had been stealing apples in
the orchard. While the other children managed to escape, the care-
taker grasped the girl and assaulted her. The incident made the
girl insane, and her obscene dance represented the sexuality which
the rape incident unleashed in her. Sexuality then, especially in
women, is associated with insanity and death; it is a side of life
with which Haukli feels completely unable to cope.

     About his own emotions for Alice, Haukli explains: "I loved
her less as a woman than as a madonna."[39] He wished Alice to be a
pure, spiritual being, but the sound of her slippers in the hall
reminded him of her erotic nature. He therefore attempted to forget the real Alice in order to retain his dream. In fact, Haukli
knew that were he to gain Alice's love, he would lose his dream.
The only woman who, in Haukli's eyes, incarnated the dream, was his
sister, and in his dream world the two women tend to melt into one:
"I took both Alice and my anguish along in my dream of forests and
mountains in Norway. She has accompanied me on paths and mountain
pastures where you and I used to walk. I soon discovered that it
became more peaceful when I lay there concentrating my thoughts on
her."[40]

     While Haukli could provoke and control the image of Alice in
his daydreams, his night dreams were completely beyond his control.
One evening he dreamed he was drowning in the sea. A boat passed
by: "In the boat sat Alice, William Lee and Alexander Selkirk.
The engine was humming. They looked at me like strangers. When
they were at some distance, Alexander Selkirk turned around slowly
and looked at me once more. He said something in his customary
tone, but even though they were by now far away, I clearly heard
every word: This is the last boat, Mr . . . .

     "The last word I refused to believe at first. He called me
Mr. Whorer, and that I am not at all. The water was gurgling in my
mouth and I drowned, since it was the last boat. Alice left on the
last boat and left me to drown."[41]

     After waking up Haukli could not rid himself of Alice's face,
the devil's face, confused with that of the female who had

frightened him so while stealing apples in Moen's orchard. There
is a relationship among apple theft, eroticism, alienation, exile,
and death in Sandemose's work. The orchard was Eden, abundant with
tempting, forbidden fruits. The face of the girl who wanted to
taste the fruit of knowledge along with the boys, only to be raped
to insanity by the worker, is an indication of Sandemose's emotions
regarding female sexuality. A longing for the pure, virgin female,
the madonna, conflicts with a strong sexual drive. While Haukli
refused to admit that his love for Alice was sexual, not spiritual,
his alter ago Alexander Selkirk unmasked its true nature: "He
called me Mr. Whorer, and that I am not at all." According to
Hareide Aarbakke the word Whorer (Norwegian "Horkarl") probably
surfaces in the dream because of the English pronunciation of
Haukli.[42] Both Alice and Selkirk refer to the protagonist as Mr.
Hahkl. While this reading may seem farfetched, it nevertheless
has some credibility. Haukli wanted to possess Alice sexually, but
without losing his image of her as an angel in flight. He realized
that for this to happen, nothing short of a miracle would have to
take place. In another dream his father appeared in order to dis-
courage the son, pleading with him to give up hoping for "the fairy
tale which cannot be realized."[43] Haukli desired Alice to save him
from himself: "I am a doubter, but I was sure from the first time
I saw her that with her I could live happily for the rest of my
life. I no longer believed that I could perish."[44] What becomes
crystal clear in the drowning dream is that Alice had absolutely no
interest in becoming Haukli's savior. She preferred the uncompli-
cated sexual advances of Selkirk and Lee to the problem-ridden
worship of Haukli. In fact, Haukli didn't interest her at all,
something he instinctively sensed. In Haukli's dream Alice made no
move to pull him into the boat: "The water was gurgling in my
mouth and I drowned, since it was the last boat. Alice left on the
last boat and left me to drown."

Alice's refusal to save Haukli represents the modern woman's
lack of sympathy for the myths men have created and imposed upon
her. Alice was not ashamed of her sexuality, and she did not see
herself as a madonna at all. Instead of lifting Haukli out of the
ugly reality of the present and help him return to the world of
Edenic innocence, she would reappear in a vision later in the novel
to show him a frightening, dead world: "It was just withering away
because it had lost its soul, its people." The narrator traces the
beginning of the slow death process to the eating of the apple and
subsequent expulsion of Adam and Eve from the garden of Eden. No
wonder that Haukli is longing to share the fate of Større, the man
from the stone age, who had the good fortune to live and die before
the fall from innocence and ensuing human degeneration.

The Problem of Guilt

Most critics agree that the central theme in Alice Atkinson is
Jørgen Haukli's guilt. Torben Ulrik Nissen goes so far as to
accuse Haukli of having killed Alice.[45] Such an interpretation

would follow the pattern of The Past Is a Dream as well as a number
of modern novels--Alain Robbe-Grillet's Le Voyeur, Johan Borgen's
Den røde tåken. In these novels, however, the evidence pointing
towards the protagonist appears massive, and in Den røde tåken at
least the protagonist himself ultimately relives the crime in a
vivid memory, accepting, even executing his own punishment.
Nothing similar happens in Alice Atkinson, where Haukli's thoughts
never seem to circle obsessively around the scene of Alice's death
in a London hotel room. He does, on the other hand, clearly feel
guilty of not having done anything to prevent her death, as Hareide
Aarbakke argues convincingly.[46] By placing himself at the service
of others without ever questioning what might be the result of his
acts, he has contributed to the creation of the deserted, dehu-
manized world that Alice showed him in his vision. At the very
beginning of the novel, he realized that as a spy his pieces of
information had been used to build up capital cases against other
human beings: "The rope would probably hold without the wretched
thread that I contributed, but then again it is made up of such
threads, and each of them is not less important than the straws of
hay that collectively become fodder for a horse."[47] Haukli is
guilty of complicity. A "good" citizen who was always willing to
follow orders, he never questioned his situation and never accepted
responsibility for his acts. When suspicious incidents started to
occur in his Bristol circle, Haukli found it convenient not to
intervene, since he had been told to close his eyes and never ask
questions. In the end, Haukli's lack of responsible involvement
may have led not only to the death of William Lee, but to that of
Alice as well.

     Throughout the book Haukli will attempt to push aside the
problem of personal responsibility. However, very early in the
novel he understands himself well enough to realize that, having
failed to commit himself, he is indeed guilty: "Now I understand
that I have distorted the truth because I didn't want to see that
Alice might be dead, and because I then would have to carry my part
of the guilt, even though I am the just one who does not meddle in
anything and has done nothing at all. The latter as well was a
sin."[48] The letters he writes to his sister enable him gradually
to see himself clearly. A series of crucial episodes, largely from
his recent past, surface, mixed with emotions and impressions
generated by the act of writing itself: "If one looks back upon
his life, it takes the shape of a continuous misdeed."[49]

     The process of writing eases Haukli's reluctance to reveal
himself. Thus, after having finished the long main section of the
novel, the narrator is able to send to his sister a letter which he
had written several months earlier, in February 1945, during the
night before William Lee was scheduled to be hanged. The letter
reveals Haukli's deep involvement in the case, as well as his
guilty conscience. Emotionally he was living through the night in
the cell with Lee. His spirit was with Lee, while his body
remained in his own room. The experience was so intense that it
caused him to throw up. Through his identification with Lee's

torments, Haukli may have succeeded in purging himself of his
personal guilt towards the other man. In a similar manner, by
writing about Alice and completely absorbing her into his mental
world, he is able to lighten the burden of guilt he felt for not
having done anything to prevent her death. It is interesting that
while Haukli had such a keen sense of being betrayed by Alice, it
was he who in a literal sense refused to save her. Haukli, in
fact, was guilty of being so caught up in his world of myth and
dreams that he became blinded to the problems of the real world
surrounding him.

Through his letters to his sister, Haukli succeeded in rees-
tablishing a link to his childhood: "It has been good to have you
to write to, sister, just as I had you in the old days. You
remember our cave in the old currant bushes, when you were six or
seven, and I eleven or twelve years old. You played with your
dolls and listened piously to my serial about the heroes Akke and
Dulle, which I never brought to an end. You never discovered, or
you were motherly enough not to want to hurt me by mentioning it,
that I after several months turned Akke and Dulle into the super-
hero Akkedulle."[50]   In the womb-like cave in the bushes the six-
year old girl had acted out for her brother the double role of
madonna ("listened piously") and mother ("motherly").

For the adult narrator, the shabby hotel room in Oslo serves
the same womb-like function, and even when he leaves the shelter
Haukli's relationships to others are simple and minimal ("Tora will
come along to cook"). In his self-assigned role as story-teller he
is able to control his own involvement at any time. Haukli's semi-
withdrawal is based on a fear of hurting others and being hurt by
them. That is why his last thoughts in the novel wander to Større:
"To him, and only him, I never did any harm."[51]

Notes

1. See for example Torben Ulrik Nissen, "Alice Atkinson og hennes elskere." In Om Sandemose - En rapport fra Jante, edited by Johannes Væth. Nykøbing Mors: Forfatterforlaget Attika, 1974, p. 99.

2. Verker i utvalg, VI, 116.

3. Ibid., p. 203.

4. Ibid., p. 118.

5. Ibid., p. 133.

6. Ibid., p. 115.

7. Ibid., p. 211.

8. Ibid., p. 118.

9. Ibid., p. 227. Sandemose's italics.

10. Ibid., pp. 227-28. Sandemose's italics.

11. Ibid., p. 228.

12. Ibid.

13. Ibid., pp. 118-19.

14. Ibid., p. 120.

15. Ibid., p. 238.

16. Ibid., p. 239.

17. Ibid., p. 252.

18. Ibid., p. 137.

19. Ibid., p. 144.

20. Ibid., p. 147.

21. Ibid.

22. Ibid., p. 149.

23. Ibid., p. 157.

24. Ibid., p. 123.

25. Ibid., p. 117. Sandemose's italics.

26. Ibid., p. 211.

27. Ibid., p. 179.

28. Ibid., pp. 143, 156, 175, 228, 156-57.

29. Høyt på en vinget hest, p. 221.

30. Verker i utvalg, VI, p. 223.

31. Ibid., p. 175.

32. Ibid.

33. Ibid.

34. Ibid., p. 234.

35. Ibid.

36. Ibid., p. 235.

37. Ibid., p. 236.

38. Ibid.

39. Ibid., p. 252.

40. Ibid., p. 230.

41. Ibid., p. 232.

42. Høyt på en vinget hest, pp. 221, 233.

43. Ibid., pp. 215-17.

44. Verker i utvalg, VI, p. 154. My italics.

45. See Chapter VIII, note 1.

46. Høyt på en vinget hest, pp. 222-23.

47. Verker i utvalg, VI, p. 125.

48. Ibid., p. 188. Sandemose's italics.

49. Ibid., p. 210.

50. Ibid., p. 253.

51. Ibid., p. 257.

9.

A Palm Green Island:
A Taste of Paradise

Published in 1950, <u>The Fairy Tale about the Time of King</u> <u>Rhascall the Seventeenth and about a Palm Green Island</u>, is a revised version of a novel written in the 1930s, <u>The Island of the</u> <u>Blessed</u> (<u>De saliges</u> ∅).[1] The short novel is a fairy tale, where Sandemose places his characters into an edenic setting in order to test their reactions and ability to cope with a life without material problems or psychological tension.

The story takes place in the sixteenth century, during the period of European expeditions to America in quest of gold and other precious metals. The aim of the conquistadors was of course to rob the New World of its abundant wealth and use it as a source of power in their European homelands. It was a period when possibilities seemed unlimited and human greed became legendary.

An English ship, "Gladys" of Newcastle, anchors close to a seemingly uninhabited tropical island in the South Atlantic ocean, where it suddenly is attacked by cannon fire from shore and sinks. Only two members of the crew, Claes and Eli, manage to escape in a small row-boat. Against incredible odds they avoid the range of the cannonade and succeed in climbing the rocky cliffs on an unapproachable, particularly inhospitable side of the island, sheltered from the view of those who opened fire on their ship. Their row-boat, however, is splintered against the cliffs, thus leaving the two men without any possibility of escaping from the island.

The inhabitants of the island are a group of young people and children of different colors and races led by a dangerous pirate, Veslegutten (Little Boy), and two women, the young, beautiful Leonora and her old helper, Black Gertrude. We learn that fifteen

years previously Vestlegutten had abducted Leonora and her younger
brothers from their home in Scotland. He was himself the victim of
human violence and brutality. Yet paralleling a hatred of adults,
Veslegutten nourishes a passionate love of children, and dreams of
creating a sheltered paradise for them: "With children you can
create a good world, I thought."[2] He believes himself predestined
to accomplish his aim, and the island society is the realization of
his dream: "I wanted to reconstruct the paradise which Our Lord
abandoned. It was to become the island of the blessed."[3]

     The island society is indeed paradise for its inhabitants.
Sheltered from evil, they retain their innocence. However, the
cost is high, since their happiness is built upon exclusion and
secrecy. No stranger must ever be permitted to land and no ship
which has entered its harbor must be permitted to leave for fear of
exposing the island society to the world beyond. While Veslegutten
is off on one of his expeditions, Leonora and Black Gertrude are
protecting the island. Any ship that approaches is attacked and
destroyed. The school of greedy sharks that inhabit the waters
surrounding the island devour all survivors.

     Built upon violence in the first place, the island society
continues to exist only through violence: "A sunny people, a
blissful people, who were playing and dancing on the beach--once
the blood had washed away and the cannons were silenced."[4] The
idea that an earthly paradise is possible only if a few selected
individuals wall themselves in and, if necessary, brutally remove
any outsider who might attempt to enter, is not unique for
Sandemose. Other writers interested in utopias have frequently
reached similar conclusions.[5] The exclusion is based on the notion
that the outside world is pure evil. Black Gertrude reassures
Leonora who occasionally resists firing on entering ships:
"Everything out there in the world is evil. Everyone is evil!"[6]
Gertrude repeatedly has to remind Leonora that they have created
the most beautiful of all possible worlds: "I have seen the world
outside," said Gertrude. "This is the most peaceful spot on the
whole earth--the whole globe--and may God preserve it for all of
us."[7]

     However, the fifteen-year old isolation is broken when,
unknown to the women, Claes and Eli succeed in landing on the
island. The two men wend their way to a small, fertile valley surrounded by protective cliffs. A river provides them with fresh
water, abundant palm trees furnish coconuts, and wild berries grow
everywhere. Occasionally, goats and chickens wander into the
valley, enabling the men to set up a primitive farm. From a lookout post in the cliffs they observe the plain where the islanders
live: "They were playing on the beach, often naked or in colorful
clothes. Then they ran and disappeared behind the palm trees."[8]

     Claes and Eli have indeed landed in paradise. The island
itself is compared to a warm, loving mother, anxious to welcome
home her two sons who have been sailing the seven seas: "The rocky

island lay there round and gentle with its many green domes, alive in the sunny haze."⁹ The cliff which the half-dehydrated sailors had to scale to view the valley below turns into a maternal breast offering to quench their thirst: "Long after sleep has extinguished their consciousness, they were still mechanically turning their heads licking--like babies by a mother's breast."¹⁰ The wind blowing through the palm trees produces a gentle lullaby, announcing that the restless adults have returned to childhood peace and harmony.

Far away from the sterile, frozen plains of Labrador, the island offers Claes and Eli all they could possibly desire in order to live happily ever after. While Leonora's peace must be periodically shattered by her involvement in shooting down all approaching strangers, Claes and Eli may live out their innocence. The cliffs around their valley form a natural fort, which they need not defend, since no humans can ever reach their side of the island. From the fort they are able to see the beach without any danger of being spotted themselves. They build a primitive shelter, eat the fruits of the earth, and expose their bodies to the pleasant, life-giving warmth of the sun. Time appears to have stopped: "They were blooming in eternal youth in the garden of paradise . . . Time became eternal."¹¹

Yet Claes and Eli are not altogether happy. Above all, curiosity persists about what is happening on the other side of the island. Unlike Leonora's discontent, which was caused by her role in defense of the island, that of Claes and Eli is wholly psychological. Eli, the younger and simpler of the two men, is also the happier: "Here it was as wonderful as any human could wish, he thought."¹² Sensing a growing sexual unrest in his companion, however, Eli is afraid that one day a woman will appear on the scene and take Claes away from him. Moreover, Eli himself starts to dream about the women he perceives down on the beach: "They had flowers in their long hair. Eli imagined that he was walking hand-in-hand in the soft grass with one of them. She and he would only watch the flowers and ocean, listen to the wind and the birds, but preferably not say anything--then everything would be spoiled."¹³ Sandemose may be telling us here that language corrupts, that the immediacy of experience is lost as language enters the scene.

More restless than Eli is Claes, who senses that their fortress is in fact a prison. His curiosity about the people on the beach keeps growing until it becomes a genuine obsession: "The thought entered Claes's mind every day that one night he had to go down there."¹⁴ Claes's unrest reaches a climax the day he discovers and excavates a gigantic statue of gold from the ground. The statue represents a primitive god, which had probably been constructed hundreds of years ago by an unknown group of people who had then inhabited Claes's and Eli's paradise: "The idol had a mighty hair of wriggling snakes, each with a small head and eyes of precious stones, raw and glowing rubies."¹⁵

The discovery of the golden idol has a profound effect on
Claes. For the first time in his life, power, which, he believes,
can be bought for gold, is within his reach. His dreams are particularly revealing in this respect. Claes's dreams focus on
women, and reveal a sadistic desire to conquer and humiliate them:
"On the beach beautiful girls were waiting--let them wait. One of
them came to him a few times. He didn't know who she was, but
thought he knew her. She was large and lovely. One night she came
and lay down on a bed next to him. It was a little lower than his
bed, for he was an important man, who could not have a woman on the
same level as he was. He stretched his head over the edge and
looked at her."[16] Hareide Aarbakke believes that the dream reveals
Claes's desire to humiliate women, perhaps because he himself has
felt humiliated by them.[17] Later, when Claes and Eli descend to
the beach and peer into the women's cabin, he realizes that the
woman from his dream is Leonora. Beset by power hunger and sexual
unrest, Claes no longer is able to find peace in his fortress.
During a visit that Veslegutten pays on the women, Claes, still
accompanied by Eli, steals the pirate's boat and ultimately returns
to England. He seeks out king Rhascall and persuades him to furnish an armed ship and crew permitting Claes to return to the
island and claim its wealth for the king. Behind Claes's dream of
power, however, is his dream of conquering Leonora, and once that
is accomplished, to conquer other beautiful, powerful women in
exotic lands. The king, weighed down by debts and a wife he no
longer loves, is receptive to Claes's tales, and he too starts
dreaming of the island paradise: "Finally he fell asleep and
dreamed he was lying in a hut made of leaves on The Island of the
Blessed. There was a wine cask by his bed, and lovely girls were
waiting in the background."[18]

Claes, made duke of Glascow and royal admiral, puts down a
plot against him by the ship's captain and conquers the island from
Veslegutten. Faced with defeat, the pirate has a crisis of consciousness, admits that his attempt to recreate paradise was
nothing but "the happy dream of a madman,"[19] and commits suicide by
wandering into the shark-infested ocean. Claes wins Leonora, while
Eli falls in love with one of the maidens from the beach. Finally,
the whole group returns to England, where they will presumably re-
enter the real world far away from the beautiful island.

While A Palm Green Island was meant to be read as a fairy
tale, the ideas expressed in the book are serious.[20] Once more
Sandemose illustrates the corrupt nature of society. King Rhascall
(the name speaks for itself) is concerned with satisfying his personal thirst for gold and women. In his childhood Veslegutten was
the victim of the Moorish army that had invaded his native Spain.
Social groups function according to the principle of the strong
tyrannizing the weak. In A Palm Green Island all the protagonists
dream of creating a better world. The purest of the dreamers is
Veslegutten, whose island paradise lasts for fourteen years. Moreover, Veslegutten's relationship to Leonora is paternal, built upon
spiritual love rather than erotic hunger. Nonetheless, Veslegutten

is a fanatic who avoids no excess in defense of his dream of the perfect society. In the end he loses out, because the people who share his paradise do not share his commitment. Leonora reacted emotionally against the attacks on the ships and sailors, and she had to be reassured constantly that the end justified the means. Leonora is betrayed by her own humanity, and Veslegutten's idealism is doomed because it is inhuman in its one-sided commitment to a dream.

Likewise, Claes fails to settle down in paradise with Eli because his greed and sexual desire prevail over his awareness that his life with Eli on the island represents the summit of human happiness: "Hear how it whistles in the palm trees! Hear the insects! Hear, the wild rooster is crowing. Hear how it whispers of peace and quiet! The ocean, which hammers against the cliffs, has to leave the island alone. Settle down, you boundlessly happy man!"[21] Happiness and peace are indeed possible, as Claes will later realize, when "sex, money and gordian knots" are kept out of one's life.[22] In fact, eroticism, greed, and violence are always placing human happiness in jeopardy. Violence was the very condition upon which Veslegutten's paradise was built. Claes's sexuality makes him wish that Eli were a woman, and Leonora is within sight to disturb his peace of mind. The soil of the island itself has become the hiding place of the golden idol, which places within Claes's reach the wealth and power he is thirsting for. The perfect society cannot be constructed in this world because it is at odds with basic human cravings. All the protagonists in the novel realize this at the end. Veslegutten, true to his ideal, takes his own life, while the less committed and less fanatic characters all return to the imperfect world of compromise and change.

Notes

1. The edition I am using was published by Det Schønbergske
Forlag, Copenhagen 1976. It is a Danish translation of the
original Norwegian version of the novel, Oslo 1950.

2. En palmegrøn ø, p. 153. I am using the Norwegian version of
the pirate's name, "Veslegutten," instead of the Danish "Lillefyr."

3. Ibid., p. 154.

4. Ibid., p. 81.

5. Thomas More's Utopia is situated on an island, Voltaire's
"Eldorado" is surrounded by almost unsurmountable cliffs, and
Sartre's "cité du soleil" in Le Diable et le bon Dieu is built
wholly on the principle of exclusion.

6. En palmegrøn ø, p. 27.

7. Ibid., p. 29.

8. Ibid., p. 44.

9. Ibid., pp. 34-35.

10. Ibid., p. 40.

11. Ibid., p. 51.

12. Ibid.

13. Ibid.

14. Ibid., p. 44.

15. Ibid., pp. 46-47.

16. Ibid., p. 55.

17. Høyt på en vinget hest, pp. 238-39.

18. En palmegrøn ø, p. 112.

19. Ibid., p. 153.

20. In "En torpedo under arken" Johannes Væth discusses briefly
the genesis of Sandemose's fairy tale. På sporet af Sandemose, pp.
130-31.

21. En palmegrøn ø, p. 56.

22. Ibid., p. 84.

10.

The Werewolf: Felicia's Dream

In the two books centered around Felicia Venhaug, The Werewolf (1958) and Felicia's Wedding (1961), Sandemose once more takes up the themes of Alice Atkinson and Her Lovers: longing for love, female sexuality, the conflicting drives towards solitude and the world. In terms of structure, however, the later novels differ significantly from the earlier one. Alice Atkinson is a tightly built work, containing holes that the reader must struggle to fill. No interpretation of the novel is likely ever to become definitive.

On the other hand, The Werewolf and Felicia's Wedding are loosely contrived. In both novels the narrator is Erling Vik, a successful writer around sixty, who must take stock of his life following the apparent murder of his lover, Felicia Venhaug: "'Look here,' I will say. 'I've been sitting at Old Venhaug and have written down all that happened in Felicia's time, about Norway in peace and Norway at war, as seen by Erling from Rjukan.'"[1] As with The Past Is a Dream and Alice Atkinson, The Werewolf is a sort of chronicle set against the backdrop of World War II. However, in the latter case the focus is on the post-war years.

The structure of The Werewolf resembles that of Erling's dreams: ". . . he seemed to have passed through several age periods, not chronologically, but round and about in his ages."[2] The novel consists of fragments that surface in Erling's mind while he is writing, as he attempts to understand himself and his rela-tionship to the presumably deceased Felicia. Felicia's Wedding describes an amalgam of Erling's thoughts and memories on a flight from Stockholm. Erling is returning home. After completion of the first book about Felicia, Erling felt a need to relive in his mind the war years, which he had spent with her in Sweden. Exception

made for the first page of the book, where we are told that
Erling's plane is ready to leave Stockholm, and the last, where the
plane is circling the Oslo Fjord, the present never intrudes upon
the past, thus perhaps weakening the novel as a journey towards
self-discovery.

To a large extent both The Werewolf and Felicia's Wedding deal
with the same characters and themes, while focusing on different
periods in Erling's life. Though loose and fragmented, Felicia's
Wedding nevertheless illuminates certain significant areas in
attempting to understand Erling's character; and it reiterates certain themes of The Werewolf. Having terminated The Werewolf, it
appears likely that Sandemose felt he had not exhausted his
material. Consequently he wrote a sequel. To my mind the finished
product would have gained in impact had the author chosen to weld
the material into one novel.[3] This fact notwithstanding, The
Werewolf has become recognized as one of Sandemose's most significant novels, an important statement about the problems with which
he had been groping throughout a lifetime. Moreover, at this stage
of his life, Sandemose was even less interested than before in
writing novels per se. In The Walls Around Jericho he explains
that what fascinates him is the present, "with cause, background,
and continuity."[4] And he continues: "I have never cared much
about novels at all, and it is boring to write them."[5] The novel
form permitted him to deal with complex psychological and social
problems he was unable to consider in other means of expression.
In other words, for Sandemose the content of the work was clearly
more important than the form. This chapter will focus upon The
Werewolf. Instead of treating Felicia's Wedding as an independent
work, I shall simply use it in order to illuminate the earlier
novels.

The setting for The Werewolf is Norway in 1958. Though the
war ended over a decade earlier, the novel's characters continue to
live in its shadow. Attitudes towards human life, for instance,
still have a violent tinge, largely guided by principles of murder
and revenge. Led by Felicia Venhaug, a group of people are
attempting to establish a small society built upon the principles
of sexual and emotional freedom. In every way the Venhaug group
represents the obverse of Jante. At Venhaug individuals grow and
expand, instead of being crippled by a conforming, negative
environment which has neither room nor tolerance for deviation from
the "Jante Law." By no means, however, is the Venhaug experiment
an unqualified success. At the conclusion of The Werewolf, Felicia
appears to have been murdered and her rather unorthodox social
group has been transformed into a conventional family. In the
dream of the narrator/protagonist Erling Vik, however, Felicia continues to live, and he sets out to compose his chronicle of her
life. Sandemose tells us, it seems, that Felicia's project was
ahead of her time. As long as the dream is kept alive, however,
hope for its realization exists.

The Plot

Because of its complexity, the plot of The Werewolf is difficult to summarize. Erling Vik, the protagonist, is the son of a
poor tailor from Rjukan. While little information is given about
Erling's relationship to his parents, he refers repeatedly to the
physical deformities of his forebears: "His limping, bald father
with his wild beard, his deaf mother with her crooked neck, and his
mother's father who lived with them and who had no hands."[6] Yet
Erling's father was a pretentious man, who liked to express his
opinions on political matters: "Vik the Tailor used an amazing
formal language, interspersed with many home-made words. People
would bring him garments to patch; and when they emerged from the
little cubby-hole where he sat looking so important they would
spread his political observations about."[7] As so often is the case
in Sandemose's fiction, the physical shortcomings symbolize psychological deformities: "Their childhood and early youth had been a
ghost-world, no less so in retrospect; semidark, damp, unreal, a
sort of small community of mentally defective demons, reminding one
of jackals in a cemetery at night, digging for corpses . . ."[8]
Much of Erling's life is, in fact, a rebellion against the atmosphere in his childhood home, assuming the form of antagonism
towards his elder brother, Gustav. While Erling broke away by
becoming an artist with little concern for the moral and sexual
norms of the majority of Norwegian society, Gustav accepted to live
by the social rules. He married, and became a construction worker
skilled in the use of dynamite, who took pride in having his financial affairs in order. Gustav is a true descendent of Jante, con-
demning his younger brother's unconventional life style, weakness
for alcohol, and lack of a "real" occupation. He seems to be a
reincarnation of Espen's brother, Petrus, in A Fugitive Crosses His
Tracks.

Despite his bohemian ways Erling is clearly marked by his
social background. The two women who will influence his life most
profoundly are both members of a higher social class. Gulnare, a
young girl he meets and knows briefly during 1915, when she was
fourteen and he was sixteen, is the daughter of a high school principal. Felicia, who first enters his life in 1934, comes from a
wealthy upper class Oslo family. The first meeting with Gulnare,
"the girl with the fairy-tale name," is described as an idyllic
initiation to female innocence, holding out the promise of future
happiness. Erling and Gulnare enjoy walks, little picnics paid for
by her allowance, and snoop at each other during skinny-dip exer-
cises in the sea. Erling dozes in Gulnare's lap, and she kisses
him. Their sexual experience never exceeds this, however. For
Erling, Gulnare's presence nevertheless bears the potential of a
healthy sexuality, in sharp contrast to what he had observed and
even participated in at Rjukan. Unfortunately, the possibility of
eternal bliss fails to materialize. Four weeks after the two met
by a store window in Oslo, Gulnare vanishes from Erling's life. In
spite of his desperate efforts to find her, Gulnare does not reappear until more than thirty years later, in an Oslo restaurant.

Having turned into a conventional, middle-aged woman, the widow of
Kortsen, a Nazi killed by the Resistance during the war, Gulnare is
barely recognizable to Erling. On the other hand, she recognizes
him and insinuates herself upon him, with accusations of his having
attempted to seduce her three decades earlier. She reveals her
gratitude towards her parents for having discovered the budding
love affair and having ended it through a whipping. The adult
Gulnare is convinced that her parents saved her from profound evil.
On the other hand Erling's whole life was profoundly marked by his
adolescent experience with Gulnare. The hope she instilled in him,
followed by her disappearance, set the tone for his future relationships with women in a manner similar to Agnes's influence on
John Torson in The Past Is a Dream.

When Erling meets Felicia Ormsund for the first time in 1934,
she is seventeen and a virgin. He is a married man of thirty-five.
Still embittered by the loss of Gulnare nineteen years earlier,
Erling seduces Felicia and vanishes from her life. His little war
with the female sex advances as he makes another woman pregnant.
His child is called Julie. When he meets Felicia for the second
time in Stockholm during the war he is divorced. By now Felicia is
a wartime refugee living with Steingrim Hagen, a friend of
Erling's, but more than willing to resume her interrupted affair.
Impulsively she marries another refugee in Sweden, Jan Venhaug, a
well-off farmer. While Steingrim commits suicide, Erling and
Felicia again take up their affair. After the war Erling spends a
considerable amount of time at Venhaug, where Julie comes as well,
a kind of adopted daughter of Felicia's.

In 1958, however, the little community is shattered when
Felicia is apparently murdered under mysterious circumstances. She
disappears, leaving a trace of bloody garments in the snow. The
Venhaug people suspect that her death is somehow linked to the war.
Felicia's younger brothers had been in the Resistance. The Nazis
caught and killed them; and Felicia took charge of the revenge by
killing Gulnare's husband, the Nazi Kortsen. In The Werewolf, and
especially in Felicia's Wedding it becomes clear that Felicia's
death in part has implicated Gulnare Kortsen. After Felicia's disappearance Jan insists that the chain of revenge must not be
broken, and he urges Erling to kill Torvald Ørje, another former
Nazi. Erling consents but he arrives too late. Tor Anderssen, the
gardener at Venhaug, who had been erotically attracted to Felicia
as well, takes on the task. Erling arrives to find Torvald Ørje
dead in his apartment.

Soon after the murder of Felicia, Jan marries Julie, while
Erling settles down at Venhaug to write his book about what "happened in Felicia's time." Once his task has been completed, he
hopes to return to a house he himself owns in a place called
Erlingvik. In Felicia's Wedding we learn that the book Erling had
set out to write is finished, and he appears to be residing permanently at Erlingvik. It is clear, however, that the writing of The
Werewolf did not completely liberate Erling from his past. He has

just visited Sweden, presumably to revisit the places where his
love affair with Felicia had matured during the war years.
Felicia's Wedding, consequently, deals largely with the years in
Sweden and with Erling's state of mind during that crucial period
in his life. The narrative is broken with descriptions of his
peaceful, solitary life in Erlingvik.

The Felicia books take up Sandemose's obsession with the
struggle between life-forces and death-forces, between the "werewolf" that exists within all of us, and the humane, generous side
of the psyche. While most of the events in The Werewolf occur
during the period immediately preceding Felicia's death in 1958,
the characters live in the shadow of the Occupation. Atrocities,
revenge, and retribution remain constant realities for most of the
characters in the novel. Thus it is made clear that Felicia's presumed murder represents part of a chain which originated during the
war years. Lives are controlled by primitive forces which civilization and peace have not succeeded in breaking down. These
aspects of The Werewolf bring to mind the context of the Icelandic
family saga, with its rigid demand for blood revenge, and give the
novel a strange, deterministic quality. Evil forces are seen
beyond the control of individuals. Though surfacing during World
War II, and dominant in all wars, their roots are found deep in the
history of our civilization. Sandemose dealt with this problem in
his very first book, Tales from Labrador. In times of peace, these
primitive elements, the "werewolf" forces, manifest themselves
covertly in society, creating what Sandemose most frequently refers
to as the Jante spirit. In times of war they are more openly
recognized and legalized, as they were in the society of the
Icelandic sagas.

Felicia's Utopia

The Werewolf describes Felicia's attempt to construct a
utopian society at Venhaug, a human community whose members are
able to live together passionately and emotionally, yet without
jealousy, hatred, and attempts to cripple each other's natural
growth. Mental and physical health, self-confidence, and tolerance
are important attributes of Felicia's ideal society, a new Eden.
Felicia's fantasy originated in an experience she had when she was
fifteen years old, during a visit to the greenhouse of an old
gardener near her home at Slemdal by Oslo: "She had been greatly
taken by the artificial summer in there and had made a long visit
with the old, white-haired man who was pruning plants."[9]

The old gardener showed Felicia the fearless, confident relationship that under the right circumstances can exist between a
human being and the world of nature. The bees in his greenhouse
did not sting but merely sat on the old man's hand, while the birds
showed absolutely no signs of fear. The gardener, however, admitted that certain ecological precautions had to be taken in order to
retain the edenic harmony. The birds must be kept in a large cage

when bees were in the greenhouse, in order to prevent them from
eating the insects. He explained to Felicia the reproductive patterns of bees and flowers: "He explained to her about pollination,
and here in the little greenhouse's concentrated sample of nature
she understood at once all that had been completely incomprehensible when her teacher had made her poetical allusions. But then,
the gardener was telling her facts, calmly and directly, as if
speaking to an equal who just didn't know the facts."[10]
Unassumingly the old gardener taught Felicia the most important
lesson of her life and provided her with nourishment for her
fantasy: "At the same time, but without having formulated it in so
many words, she had learned what it meant to adjust oneself to
life's demands in one's own little circle and be happy there."[11]
She toys with the idea of becoming a gardener herself, but gives it
up in favor of a more challenging project: to create around herself a controlled environment patterned upon that of the Slemdal
greenhouse. She realizes, however, that in order to succeed, she
must proceed with caution, exercise discretion in selecting the
members of the group and constantly watch their development: "He
told her that these were especially friendly bees, and at first she
had thought that he was making fun of her, but he went on ex-
plaining that there was a great difference in the temperament of
the bees from hive to hive. 'All come from a single queen,' he
said, 'and if her disposition is unfriendly, then this trait is
inherited by all her descendants, but if she is friendly then her
children are friendly too. That is my explanation, but animals are
like people—you can't be too sure about anything.'"[12]

The old gardener thus admits that even in the most perfectly
planned environment things can go wrong and misfits appear to spoil
the harmony. Nevertheless, the lesson Felicia learns in the
Slemdal greenhouse will have a far-reaching effect upon her life,
since she applies it to the ideal family she herself is planning to
raise. Seen in this context it becomes clear why Felicia, though
she loves the alcoholic, undependable Erling Vik, choses to marry
the stable, mild-mannered Jan Venhaug. While Erling remains her
lover, she wants to be absolutely sure that any child she bears
will carry the Venhaug genes and heritage. In fact, when she
wishes to become pregnant, she makes sure to remove Erling from the
scene several months in advance. The docile Jan not only possesses
a temperament which Felicia finds congenial; he also is the heir to
Venhaug, the great farm which has been in the hands of his family
for generations. Jan's background and Felicia's inherited wealth
should then provide the best possible soil for her garden. Once
more Sandemose reveals his belief that the lower classes had been
too damaged to form the nucleus of a society built upon trust,
sexual liberty, and tolerance. By way of contrast the best bet lay
in the shared values and inherited traditions of the old Norwegian
farm aristocracy. One need only recall Stein and Maja in A Sailor
Goes Ashore and Emil and Vera in September.

Superficially, Felicia's experiment appears to be a success.
Her husband, Jan, not only tolerates Erling Vik's frequent visits

to Venhaug, but also joins Felicia in urging Erling to move there
permanently; and a solid friendship appears to develop between the
two men.[13]   Felicia brings to Venhaug Erling's young daughter,
Julie, reared in an orphanage and well on her way to becoming a
human wreck. Transplanted, Julie regains her mental and physical
health and grows into a beautiful, harmonious young woman. The
narrator compares her to a plant, which having been removed from
unhealthy soil, reroots itself naturally and begins to thrive.
Felicia's own children are happy and healthy, in contrast to the
unfortunates of Sandemose's earlier works. Finally, aunt Gustava,
an old woman from the area, is incorporated into the group, which
with three generations thereby becomes complete (five, in fact, if
one considers that Julie is in her early twenties, Jan and Felicia
in their forties, and Erling around sixty).

Beneath the pleasant surface, however, dangers lurk. Chief
among them is the threat of the "werewolf," the principle of evil.
This threat to harmony may be existential, psychological, or, as so
often in Sandemose's work, social: "There is something that can't
bear for people to be happy,"[14] Jan explains to Erling after
Felicia's disappearance and presumed death. Jealousy, intolerance
of the happiness of others, is a constant obstacle. The most ominous threat derives from the individuals themselves. None of the
characters in the novel has completely succeeded in destroying the
"werewolf" within.

Jan Venhaug

The most civilized character in The Werewolf is Jan. Des-
cended from a long line of prosperous farmers, Jan is a social
insider, a "man of luck," the one Felicia chooses as husband and
father of her children. Pointing to the similarity between their
first names, Carl-Eric Nordberg calls Jan "a refined successor of
John Wakefield."[15]   Unlike John, who fell victim to Espen's rage at
Misery Harbor, Jan is a survivor. Whatever happened to him,
Felicia once predicted, Jan would patiently start reconstructing
his life. After Felicia's death, and after Erling Vik has with-
drawn from active life, Jan picks up the pieces of Felicia's dream,
marries Julie, and starts building a new family unit at Venhaug. A
person who never doubts his place in the world, Jan nevertheless
has the capacity to recognize his mistakes and learn from them. As
a youth, Jan had fallen hopelessly in love with Vigdis, the daughter of a small shopkeeper. A typical Jante person, Vigdis was stupid, discontented with her lot, snobbish, and domineering. Scorn-
ful of farmers, she dreamt of marrying Jan, selling Venhaug, and
moving to the city. Vigdis had no potential for growth, and
Felicia, upon running into her twenty-five years later, is struck
by how aged she looks. Vigdis is a woman who entraps men with her
body. Once the body's beauty fades, such a person is left with
nothing, ". . . for it requires a mind to retain one's youth."[16]
Agnes in The Past Is a Dream is an example of this type of woman as
well.

Jan's love for Vigdis had been marked by agony and humiliation: "Jan told about his consuming jealousy, nights without
sleep, derision and broken promises."[17]   Retrospectively he recalls
their affair as a strictly physical phenomenon: "In other words,
it was all strictly animal?" Erling asks him, and Jan confirms,
"Strictly animal. You hit it right, and there is something wrong
when a woman is useful only for mounting."[18]   Nevertheless, the
humiliations he suffers at the woman's hand ultimately reach their
limit. Jan will go no further, and breaks off an affair which had
become immersed in stupidity, distrust, and jealousy. Vigdis
learns nothing from the experience, while Jan on the other hand
begins to comprehend the enslaving character of pure sexual attraction: "I can imagine that the sexual part amounts to sixty or
seventy percent of the value, as a matter of fact. But the other
thirty percent should also be there."[19]   In marrying Felicia, beautiful, intelligent, and willful, Jan had acted in accordance with
what previous experience had taught him: "Jan had drawn the logical conclusions from his experience with her (Vigdis), and had
built something that stood up better. Like an architect, he had
seen mistakes in the old building and not repeated them."[20]   Above
all, "the jealousy finally burned itself out."[21]   Clearly remaining
sexually attracted to Felicia until her death, Jan nevertheless is
able to welcome Erling to Venhaug, accept him as his wife's lover,
and participate in a friendship which appears solid among the members of the triangle.

Jan is open, tolerant, and unafraid to admit that the "werewolf" continues to live inside him, but he will not permit the
beast to control him. Felicia calls Jan "the most innocent person
I know."[22]   When he sees what is reputed to be Felicia's blood on
the snow, he faints with emotion, an act that no man from Jante
would permit himself to do. Shortly after Felicia's disappearance
he admits to having entered Julie's room during the night because
he could not tolerate remaining in the dark alone. Felicia surely
would have understood, he reassures himself. Jan's psychological
harmony extends to a refusal to tolerate evil. During the war he
was an ardent patriot, willing to participate in the liquidation of
Norway's enemies. He took the lives of others, it is true, but
never enjoyed it. To his mind the most repulsive Nazi remained a
human being. On the negative side, Jan is unable to forgive his
enemies even after the end of the war. Convinced that Felicia's
death is retribution for her killing of Kortsen several years earlier, Jan refuses to let the matter rest. He insists on revenge.

In a memorable scene Erling and Julie are sitting in the big
living room at Venhaug. On the wall hang two large pictures of
Felicia's brothers who were killed by the Nazis. In the corner is
a picture of a man with a German shepherd. Jan suddenly enters the
room drinking from a bottle he is holding in his hand: "He looked
up at the enlarged photographs of Harald and Bjørn whom the Germans
had murdered. Julie and Erling could not see his face. A few
times he drank from the bottle. After perhaps a quarter of an hour
he rose and kicked over the bottle; with the sound of a faintly

gurgling brook the contents emptied on the floor, spreading an odor
of cognac through the room. Then Jan said, in a low, clear voice:
'She avenged you.'"[23] He then turns and leaves the room, shutting
off the lights as he retreats. In tears Julie huddles closer to
Erling, who proceeds to turning on the reading lamp: "From the
corner of the house the man with the police dog looked at them,
expressionless."[24]

The scene is significant. Jan seems to believe that he cannot
let Felicia's apparent murder go unavenged. As Felicia had avenged
her brother, Jan must now see to it that her murder is properly
avenged. Alcohol will assist in breaking down his rational side
and make the bestial one surface for the occasion. Normally, Jan
rarely drinks. As Erling explains to Julie, before the pictures of
her dead brothers Jan has solemnly promised Felicia revenge. The
figure with the police dog represents Jan the hunter. That he is
pictured with a dog rather than a wolf is nonetheless significant,
suggesting that Jan will possibly control the beast within.

Subsequently, Jan asks Erling to carry out the revenge, citing
as his own principal responsibilities care of the farm, Felicia's
children, and Julie, whom he wishes to marry. For the sake of the
future, Jan refuses to risk his life. His responsibility is to
safeguard the Venhaug heritage for future generations. Whether or
not Jan's motivation is honest is impossible to tell from the text.
However this may be, Jan's request reminds Erling of his own outsider status. He is expendable and had deluded himself if ever he
had thought otherwise. Whatever the outcome, Erling decides to
leave Venhaug forever and packs his bags. After discovering that
someone else, the gardener Tor Anderssen, decided to take the
revenge into his own hands, Erling reverses his decision. Unlike
Jan and Erling, who decide upon a course of action after carefully
scrutinizing the situation, Tor follows his instincts blindly. In
him, more clearly than in any of the other characters in the novel,
the wolf is in control.

The Werewolf and the Knight

In The Werewolf the Sandemose protagonist has in a sense been
split into two, the writer Erling Vik and the gardener Tor
Anderssen; both are erotically attracted to Felicia. According to
the critic Jostein Soland, Erling is capable of bringing out the
positive side of Felicia's sexuality, while Tor's influence on her
is wholly negative.[25] The name Tor, of course, immediately stamps
the gardener as a "name without luck," while Erling is traditionally the name of a leader. In The Werewolf Tor Anderssen is frequently referred to as a goblin or a wolf, while Erling is a
knight. Throughout the novel Felicia is indirectly pleading with
Erling to save her from the goblin, who appears to hold a magic
power over her. Erling, unfortunately, is unwilling or unable to
play out his role as knight for Felicia, and by so doing prevents
her from living a happy, harmonious life.

Tor is a typical Jante individual, dull, unimaginative, and stupid. Always on his guard against others, he is supersensitive to ridicule. He hates to be laughed at, and will never forget the slightest personal criticism. Because some Germans were making fun of him as he slipped on a sidewalk in Oslo in 1940, Tor Anderssen became a committed enemy of the Nazis: "Tor Anderssen became an avenging angel, completely heartless, strong as a pile-driver, and with the courage of a pile-driver."[26] His personality, however, is such that he would have been more at home on the other side: "Neither Jan nor Felicia--Erling was somewhere else--had had the slightest doubt during the war that Tor Anderssen was the born Nazi; through a ridiculous incident he had become furious with his brothers under the skin."[27] Many years after the war, Felicia's death provided Tor with another opportunity to take revenge against his old enemies. He is indeed the unwanted hammer man, and it is important that the weapon he uses to bludgeon Torvald Ørje is an iron pipe, a kind of primitive hammer.

While Erling Vik is a far more positive character than Tor Anderssen, he lacks the liberating qualities of a Jan Venhaug. Social background is crucial. Born into a rag tailor's family of cripples, Erling, one may say, had himself suffered "birth defects." Seeing this clearly, Felicia rejects and fears this side of her lover: "She didn't want you as long as you--in one guise or another--acted like the son of a tailor. She wanted a healthy and grown Erling who no longer took all the hopeless short cuts."[28] Felicia warns Erling that an evil spirit is raging within him, namely "the Werewolf you have talked so much about."[29] She compares this spirit to a pyromaniac who is destroying Erling's mental landscape: "Somewhere within you there grows such a forest. I became aware of it in time, and took care. Other women got lost in your burned forest, where no birds were singing and no heart beating. There lay only the decayed corpse of a lame and smoke-blackened tailor."[30] Felicia desires to assist Erling in ridding himself of the haunting side of his past: "Erling, I have the most intense desire to take care of you," she tells him,[31] and repeatedly attempts to persuade him to move to Venhaug on a permanent basis.

Erling shares Felicia's humanistic vision, "the dream of a better humanity, forgiveness, good will, talks about world situations, without a knife in the sleeve, the dim dream of peace and thaw in the heart, the dream that made him long and weep."[32] As Erling sees it, the war and violence derive from unhealthy social attitudes of individuals: "He had come to the conclusion that in the enforced isolation and uncommunicativeness of the individual lay the most dangerous seed of violence and war."[33] Erling himself appears to be basically a "closed" person, an individual hiding within a strong, protective shell, yet in theory at least he is an ardent advocate of openness, tolerance, and trust. To Erling, Felicia's Venhaug embodies the realization of a dream, of a "good place," where the individual personality might thrive. When Felicia jokingly implies that it is his sexual desire for her that pushes him toward the farm, Erling replies in a tone more serious than the occasion appears to warrant: "I came for everything Venhaug stands for."[34] Venhaug offers Erling the possibility of integration within a healthy social group, devoid of the pettiness and backbiting intrinsic within the Jante law. To become a member of Venhaug, however, Erling must foresake his past, forget his origins, and erase the scars left by a painful childhood and youth. Only then will he fully belong to Venhaug.

But does Erling truly wish to break with his sources? He persistently resists Felicia's offer to settle permanently in his cottage at "Old Venhaug." Although he undoubtedly loves and admires Felicia, he cannot help seeing her as an antagonist: "They had reached the point where one knows almost everything about the other--except for the locked-up part; and then there was this undercurrent of warfare."[35] Erling fears that were he to move to Venhaug, he would not only give up his past, but his independence as well. Without saying so, Felicia would impose upon him her values--her life style, moderate drinking habits, regular meals, behavior that she considers correct. On the other hand Erling cherishes his irregular life, which is rooted (along with the Jante law) in his childhood environment--where a meal represented battling for a larger share and where alcoholism was the common means of escaping the misery of the everyday world. The description of Erling's grandfather, "that hairy, dirty parody of a human being without hands, holding the liquor bottle with the stumps of arms when he quenched his thirst," is striking.[36] When he first escaped from Rjukan for Oslo, Erling lived with an alcoholic uncle and aunt, for whom he continues to feel great affection. Never would this couple feel comfortable at Venhaug. While Erling's brother Gustav rejects alcohol for conventional respectability, still obeying the Jante law, Erling indulges in excessive drinking. His attitude towards drinking is ambivalent. On the one hand he resents Felicia's attempts to cure him of the habit; on the other, he is clearly ashamed, admitting that he never wanted to move to Venhaug because he didn't want them to see him "like that."

The mixture between indulgence and shame in Erling's attitude towards alcohol extends to his general attitude towards his past. On the one hand, he wishes nothing more than to be rid of it forever; on the other, he clings to it, defending his origins whenever someone attempts to remove them from him. With her insistence that he move to Venhaug, Felicia (so he believes) is attempting to absorb him, to erase his identity. Fear of this absorption is reflected in a yet more fundamental fear of insanity and death, which he experiences most keenly precisely when drunk. Venhaug wishes indeed to integrate Erling, but solely on its own terms. More than willing to let Erling live in a cottage on the older part of the farm, "Old Venhaug," Jan would never sell the old farm house to him. After Felicia's disappearance, Jan offers to move Erling's own house, "Erlingvik," to Venhaug. He proposes that Erling sell the house to him; in turn, Jan will permit Erling to live in it for life.

Surely Erling feels a strain of resentment towards Jan the insider and proper heir to the prosperous farm, the man who was Felicia's legal husband and the father of her children: "Jan Venhaug was fifteen years younger than he, and must have a different view on many matters. What have you actually thought, Jan, of the threads that were spun, up to the night you lay down to sleep with my daughter and made me the old pensioner on your estate?"[37] In <u>The Werewolf</u> this bitterness is generally latent. In <u>Felicia's Wedding</u>, however, Erling's true emotions towards Jan erupt in two visionary, almost surrealistic chapters.[38] In the first of them Erling and Jan are together on an island, carrying rifles. Erling challenges Jan to a duel. The latter, however, does not appear to accept, because "one could only challenge a gentleman, and that Erling was not."[39] Jan finds a brook and, before sitting down to rest, drinks from it. Meanwhile, within hearing distance of the brook, Erling is dying of thirst. The sky becomes an ocean of fire, and Erling hears a pack of howling dogs. Then Erling hears Jan calling him, and turns his rifle in the direction of the voice: "Erling sank down on his left knee and aimed in the direction of the sound. His muscles and tendons became tight as steel. He heard some fumbling steps and there was Jan, shapeless in the restless half-light. He stood there, his arms stretched out to his sides, perhaps to show that he had no weapon. Erling!

"The distance was not more than ten meters. Erling aimed at his head and fired. In the spurting flame from the barrel he saw Jan's tired face, his messy hair covering his forehead. The echo stormed through the mountains, echo upon echo gradually dying down, and the dogs became silent on the beach."[40]

The quoted passage shows Erling's suppressed resentment against Jan, his inferiority complex and his feeling of guilt vis-a-vis the other man. The howling dogs represent the "werewolf" forces inside Erling, the jealousy towards Jan that he has attempted to hold at bay. It is interesting that in the dream Jan is represented as the innocent one, attempting to call his friend repeatedly and finally appearing, weaponless. In a second visionary sequence, Jan and Erling are in a small boat, near the shore of an island. Dogs now run along the beach, but some of them enter the water and swim towards the boat. As one of the animals approaches, Erling notices its eyes: "There had been something in the eyes of the dog which had come closest to the boat, an expression that one would never behold in the eyes of a dog, a longing, a wish, a demand, the begging glance of a human being."[41] Underscored is the affinity between the dog and Erling. It is quite clear that Erling himself senses the connection, as he turns toward Jan and asks: "Jan, is there something wrong with me?

"Jan hesitated before he answered, as if he were thinking about it: 'Everything is wrong.'"[42] The description calls to mind the Klabautermann, the miserable outcast always on the lookout for a boat to join, or the story of the rat which the crew of the "Fulton" finally caught and threw into the sea, but which would

keep swimming in the hope of reaching the ship again. It is also
reminiscent of the dream in <u>Alice Atkinson</u> where Jørgen Haukli is
drowning in the sea as Alice sails past with her two lovers.
Despite the fact that Erling Vik has travelled far in his attempt
to free himself from his "Jante complex," much remains of the
proletarian boy, whose eyes express longing and desire to share of
the riches of others. Once the riches are offered him, however, he
is unable to accept.

Unlike the crew members of the "Fulton," who at any cost
wanted to rid their ship of the rat, Jan never throws Erling out of
the boat, the arch in the sea which Venhaug represents. On the
contrary, it is Erling himself who insists on leaving, in spite of
the fact that he knows that in the long run his salvation may be
found within the Venhaug community. After Felicia's disappearance,
Erling is unprepared emotionally to join forces with Jan. Nor will
he abandon completely the shattered dream Felicia had passed down
to him. Erling consequently withdraws into his own private, mental
space, which he calls Erlingvik, in order to reconstruct his life.
Erlingvik is, to be sure, a house Erling owns in a sheltered cove,
but it is as well a symbol of withdrawal into the self. Erlingvik
is a place where no humans are welcome, except as figments of
Erling's own mind: "It was sunrise from the Garden of Eden when he
rowed into Erlingvik and pulled up the boat on the shore. He stood
long and beheld his kingdom before he walked over to the three tall
white birches against the mountainside. He did not look up at the
wall on the other side where they were sitting, watching him; he
did not wish to do so before he reached the slab between the
birches. He did not bend over the slab, he felt he must first have
permission."[43] The people who were watching Erling are Felicia and
Steingrim, his two dead friends. That they are holding hands indicates that their sexuality has been transformed into childlike tenderness and love: "They were very solemn, but a great peace lay on
their faces. The closed severity was gone from Steingrim's face,
it appeared rather boy-like curious--what errand might Erling
have?"[44] Erling, in fact, has come to take possession of a golden
hammer which he had found as a child, and which he had subsequently
buried under a slab in Erlingvik. However, in order to do so, he
needs Felicia's consent, and even though he knows she is dead, he
fears that she may not approve of his action: "Carefully he
brushed off some dirt from the shining hammer and when he again
looked up at Felicia, a faint warmth was already at work in his
blood, soon to turn into an intoxication."[45]

The hammer is Erling's poetic gifts. It is also the weapon of
Thor, the outcast. Erling needs his hammer in order to be able to
write. Erling's creative talents are closely associated with his
unhappy childhood. By wanting Erling to forget about his past,
Felicia had in fact been instrumental in killing his creativity.
Erling had dug down his hammer because Felicia did not approve of
it. She of course, had never understood how significant his past
was to him as an artist. This time, however, Felicia does not
attempt to tell Erling what to do: "She must hurry now and give a

sign if she was against it, but she only watched him with her big, deep eyes. Steingrim did the same. Erling could see no motion except in Felicia's hair, when a breath of wind fluttered it."[46] It is only at this moment that Erling fully comprehends that Felicia is not trying to tell him what to do because she is indeed dead. From now on Erling will incorporate Felicia into _his_ Eden instead of being incorporated in _hers_. The feeble warmth he had sensed inside grows into a violent explosion of creative energy: "He knocked on the mountain wall with his gold hammer and called aloud: then a white, crackling light streamed over him. It rushed like floods of white horses over the broad fields, he ran from dungeon to dungeon and loosened all the ropes of dreams, hit the law's watch-dog in the head at the door, and opened the sluice gates to the springs of life; he blasted his mind to pieces, some of which floated away down the streams, while other pieces escaped like dark birds to rank heaths where they were more at home. He raised a new heaven and a new earth, but in the new-created world were also Felicia and Steingrim, this he could see as he pushed out the boat and the smoke lifted from over Erlingvik."[47] It appears then that Felicia had to die in order for Erling to regain his creative powers. The base upon which he will create his vision of the future is her splintered dream of Venhaug, the "child" she had given birth to but was unable to help grow into a strong, healthy adult. While the people surrounding Felicia, particularly Erling himself, certainly contributed to the failure of her dream, the chief obstacle was probably, as is so often the case in Sandemose's characters, within her own personality.

Felicia

The most interesting character in The Werewolf is Felicia herself. In fact, she is the only developed female character in Sandemose's entire work. Felicia's main characteristic is her open, voracious sexuality, which Erling Vik had awakened. While Gulnare's parents quenched their daughter's sexual and emotional development, Felicia's brief affair with Erling in 1934 illustrated her potential for giving of herself to others. As young girls Gulnare and Felicia were both trusting, innocent, and naturally eager to share their sexuality. Society would destroy Gulnare's potential, while Felicia developed without censure. When Erling meets her in Stockholm during the war, she is a young woman who had experienced several lovers. She offers her warmth through sex, it is true; but this is not her sole way of human sharing. She can form deep non-sexual attachments as well—to Gustava, to her children, to Erling's daughter, Julie. However, discovery of her sexuality is what awakened Felicia to others. Loss of virginity, the fall of the Madonna, had turned "chaste Felicia" into the mature woman who fails to understand why sexual love should be exclusive. Therefore, she sees no problem in loving several men at the same time, and jealousy has no place in the world she wishes to construct. In The Werewolf Gulnare represents the "old" woman, whose freedom was stunted by social restraint, while Felicia

represents the "new," liberated female. Gulnare loses her beauty
of body and spirit; Felicia's beauty and strength increase as she
grows older. Felicia never hides her age. She not only accepts
her prematurely gray hair, but turns it into a symbol of vitality:
"My connection with her dates from the time she was with Steingrim
and never ceased. Before that I had met her only once; that was in
1934, when she was seventeen. Then she was dark-haired but as can
happen with coal-black hair, there was already streaks of silver;
now she has for long worn her silver crown, without a touch of
black in it."[48] Her body exudes life and health: "Her body was
brown like a Maori's, and the color seemed even warmer in the
fluttering half-light. Her hair spread like a white bird over her
head and when the faint light struck her eyes there were sudden
gleams."[49] After her disappearance, as Erling Vik sits down to
write his book about Felicia, his attitude is one of unadulterated
adoration: "I'll try to draw a picture of her, as I see and feel
it within me and impressed on the underside of my eyelids--a
picture drawn in combat-desire but also blind admiration, drawn by
a boy standing below on the street, his head thrown back, ready to
tell of the golden girl between the towers of Oslo Town Hall--."[50]
Yet the story of Felicia is a story of failure, or at best of only
partial success.

Felicia's main problem as well as her main virtue, stems from
her sexual drive. In her relationship with Erling, Felicia is
clearly the dominant partner. After his return from Las Palmas in
1950, she drives to his home in Erlingvik in an aroused state:
"Erling was not home as yet, but someone else might see her emotion, one could never be sure. And how she was trembling as violently as she had done the first few minutes, eight years earlier,
after she had avenged her brothers, with the informer lying at her
feet. Now she was afraid she might lose control of her car; she
felt her heart swell and press her lungs against the sides of her
breast, she felt she was choking with joy and about to faint, she
groaned in futile anger as she bent forward over the steering wheel
and fought her emotion. She thought wildly and blindly that it
must stop when the shaking of the motor was stilled and no longer
could affect her, although it never had affected her before. She
bent over the wheel, kicked with her feet, bit her lips until she
tasted blood. Then it died down. She remained slumped over the
wheel, her eyes empty, until she heard another car approaching."[51]

Anticipating the reunion with Erling is sufficient to send
Felicia into an erotic frenzy. In fact her sexual drive is
directly compared to a murderous one, as Felicia associates her
orgasmic state with what she had felt just after her murder of the
Nazi Kortsen eight years earlier. This time, however, the "victim"
is absent, and it is Felicia who experiences "death" as she collapses over the steering wheel of her car. During Erling's visits
at Venhaug, it always is Felicia who comes to spend the night with
him. In fact, Felicia's sexuality is so overwhelming that it
amazes Erling, who has ambivalent feelings about it: "Erling spent
himself before Felicia and he watched her transformation--her calm

and happy face with half-open mouth and blissful smile which with a
few spasms was suddenly turned into a Medusa-like fury, a contorted
face as in labor pain. Nerves and muscles around the beautiful
eyes became lax, giving her the ugly cross-eyed look of a
changeling. Suddenly Erling was thrown aside, as when a cross-wave
hits a boat. Groaning she fumbled after him and one of her hands
managed to get hold of his hair. He was afraid he might break her
fingers--they were frozen as in a cramp--but he loosened her grip
so as not to have his hair pulled out by the roots. By now he was
sufficiently outside to appreciate the more comic aspect of what
was happening and he wondered if perhaps at last he could see a
sensible reason why people in the old days wore nightcaps.
Standing beside the bed he watched her rave on to an end, and he
recalled that the winged horse of poetry was the offspring of the
sea-god Poseidon and Medusa."[52]   Far from using sex as a means of
sharing an experience with her lover, Felicia here wishes to devour
him. She has herself become a wild beast, only wishing to still
her enormous hunger. While Erling finds Felicia slightly comical,
the problem of overwhelming, untamed sexuality is close to the core
of The Werewolf and significant in Sandemose's work in general.
Despite his ironic description, it is clear that Erling fears
Felicia's sexuality; like Felicia's demands that he belong completely to Venhaug, her demands upon his body threaten his identity
and integrity. Consequently, Erling spends long periods of time
away from Venhaug, either at Erlingvik, or else in Oslo, in the
company of women whom he is capable of controlling. The struggle
that dominates the relationship between Erling and Felicia therefore is not exclusively built upon principles of social class. It
is sexual war lurking beneath a harmonious surface. Erling's chief
weapon against Felicia is the withholding of sexual favor, normally
considered a female prerogative; his absences drive her to the
verge of madness.

Felicia attempts to sublimate her need for Erling by building
a greenhouse where exotic plants and wild birds find shelter. It
is a sensuous garden of delights in which Felicia will remove her
clothes and prance about nude. The gardener at Venhaug, Tor
Anderssen, discovers Felicia's game and finds a way of viewing her
performances through a vent. Aware of her audience, Felicia will
now perform for the gardener, initiating a strange affair without
words or physical contact. Tor is a classical misfit, and Felicia
takes advantage of his frustrated sexuality by trapping him. Naked
among her plants and birds and knowing full well that Tor is
standing by, she customarily keeps his peephole open: ". . . she
liked to torture and degrade Tor Anderssen and watch him play the
fool. Her blood would throb, she would smile enchanted, and her
eyes would glitter from something akin to hot, selfish evil, while
standing there only a foot from him, on her side of the wall."[53]
Unable to tame her own, Felicia toys with Tor's animal instincts,
keeping him in an aroused state: "I have seen him stare at her
like a beast in heat," Jan remarks.[54]   Jan is clearly aware of what
is going on, and he admits that it is not within his power to do
anything about the situation: "Jan put his hands behind his head

and looked at the ceiling: 'Sometimes there are things one knows
but can't do anything about. I would like to get rid of Tor
Anderssen. He has never had a woman and he exudes rape. He is
puritanism's farthest outpost.'"[55]

As matters occur, the beautiful, intelligent Felicia has
become as dependent upon the gardener as he is upon her. For her
Tor represents impersonal male sexuality which she can both
titillate and humiliate: "The stupid man at the ventilator represented the whole world's maleness, with a brain the size of a
dried-up walnut kernel, the male-world's collective phallus placed
the way the men themselves had managed it--helpless and suffering
at a stone wall with a peep-hole, helpless and scared, with weak
desires relieved through sadistic dreams."[56] The encounters with
Tor degrade Felicia as well, bringing to the surface her werewolf
forces: "As he began to move and cautiously approach, she pulled
back her lips like a snarling dog . . . ."[57] The narrator compares
Felicia to the princess imprisoned by a goblin in a glass mountain,
waiting for a knight to come and release her. Of course, unlike
the princess in the fairy tale, Felicia herself is far from innocent, since both she and Tor Anderssen are victims of bestial inner
forces that they neither understand nor control. Moreover,
Felicia's prison is self-constructed and she has orchestrated the
whole affair. Nevertheless, Felicia keeps hoping that her knight
will release her; the knight, of course, is incarnated in Erling
Vik, who, for reasons of his own, is unwilling to save his princess.

In one sense, The Werewolf shows Erling Vik's failure to
establish a harmonious relationship with Felicia, the modern, liberated woman. The failure is caused by psychological problems on
both sides. Felicia is unable to accept Erling as he is, while
Erling on his side is frightened by Felicia's violence and power.
He resents Felicia's sexuality and desire to take complete charge
of him. While Erling himself had awakened her sexually, he is
repelled by her eroticism. He continues to regret and dream about
young Gulnare, symbol of female purity and innocence. Only after
Felicia's disappearance, when she has become a part of Erling's
imaginary world, no longer with a physical power of exerting her
personality, does he fully accept her. It is interesting that when
she appears in his vision of Erlingvik, her sexuality has given way
to tenderness; like young adolescents Felicia and her former lover,
Steingrim, are holding hands.

Except that in the earlier books the possibility of a harmonious coexistence was never put to a test, the pattern in The
Werewolf follows that of The Past Is a Dream and Alice Atkinson.
In The Past Is a Dream Gunder Gundersen, unlike Jan Venhaug, was a
jealous man. Moreover, John Torson never really wanted to live on
a permanent basis with Susanne, because his freedom and independence were too precious to him. In Alice Atkinson Jørgen Haukli
did not have the option, since Alice showed no interest in him
whatsoever. Original to The Werewolf is the space Sandemose gives

to Felicia as a character with a personality distinctly her own. She is the only one who escapes the traditional myth of woman as madonna or whore. It is of course true that Maja in <u>A Sailor Goes Ashore</u> and Vera in <u>September</u> prepare the character of Felicia, but the author never develops their characters. Moreover, in spite of her failure to establish a harmonious relationship with Erling, Felicia is seen as an ideal woman. It is true that she does not survive, and that the safer, more conventional Julie takes her place as mistress of Venhaug, whose principal charge is the responsibility for rearing the next generation. Yet Felicia's death does not blot her out. She explained that even after her death she would continue to be present at Venhaug. It is significant that her body is never found, an indication that symbolically at least she is not really dead. No physical proof of death exists, except some bloody marks of her body in the snow, a few scattered pieces of clothing, and a hole in the ice. Subsequently a large painting of her is hung in the living-room at Venhaug joining those of her brothers, a reminder of her continued presence there. One may say that after her death, Felicia is transformed into a mythic woman, replacing the stereotypes in Erling's mind. In fact, Erling solemnly promises to remain faithful to her all his life. We learn in <u>Felicia's Wedding</u> that sexually Erling fails to keep his promise; mentally, however, the image of Felicia will dominate Erling's existence. In <u>The Werewolf</u>, Sandemose has developed a new woman, strong, erotic, intelligent. It is around her and her shattered dream of a utopian society that Erling Vik will construct his vision of the future.

Notes

1. Aksel Sandemose, The Werewolf, translated by Gustav Lannestock. Madison and Milwaukee: The University of Wisconsin Press, p. 374. See Verker i utvalg, VII, p. 382.

2. The Werewolf, p. 373. Verker i utvalg, VII, p. 381.

3. In The Walls around Jericho Sandemose explains that the material in The Werewolf was intended as a preface to a long work. However, the material grew into a long novel itself, and he wanted to use it as the first volume of a trilogy. Volumes two and three were to be called Inferno and Erling from Rjukan. He explains that "The three were planned as a unit, but the material became too overwhelming." Verker i utvalg, VIII, p. 12.

4. Ibid., p. 81.

5. Ibid.

6. The Werewolf, p. 227. Verker i utvalg, VII, p. 234. The portrait of Erling's grandfather is probably built upon that of Sandemose's own, an eccentric whose left foot was destroyed during the Danish-German war of 1864. See Nordberg, p. 15.

7. The Werewolf, p. 228. Verker i utvalg, VII, p. 235.

8. Ibid., p. 28.   Ibid., p. 33. Sandemose's italics.

9. Ibid., p. 109.   Ibid., p. 114.

10. Ibid., p. 110.   Ibid.

11. Ibid.   Ibid., p. 115.

12. Ibid., p. 109.   Ibid., p. 114.

13. In his interesting article "Et annulert drap in Felicias bryllup," Asmund Lien discusses Erling Vik's latent hostility towards Jan Venhaug. Lien bases his study on two chapters of Felicia's Wedding. Om Sandemose - En rapport fra Jante, pp. 127-40.

14. The Werewolf, p. 342. Verker i utvalg, VII, p. 350.

15. Nordberg, p. 72.

16. The Werewolf, p. 255. Verker i utvalg, VII, p. 263. Sandemose's italics.

17. Ibid., p. 230.   Ibid., p. 237.

18. Ibid., p. 231.   Ibid., p. 238.

19. Ibid.   Ibid.

20. Ibid., p. 328.   Ibid., p. 336.

21. Ibid., p. 231.   Ibid., p. 239.

22. Ibid., p. 237.   Ibid., p. 245.

23. Ibid., p. 330.   Ibid., p. 338.

24. Ibid.   Ibid.

25. Jostein Soland, "Kjærlighetsrittet i Varulven." Om Sandemose
- En rapport fra Jante, pp. 101-26.

26. The Werewolf, p. 24. Verker i utvalg, VII, p. 29.

27. Ibid.   Ibid.

28. Ibid., p. 102.   Ibid., p. 107.

29. Ibid., p. 104.   Ibid., p. 108.

30. Ibid.   Ibid.

31. Ibid.   Ibid.

32. Ibid., p. 36.   Ibid. p. 41.

33. Ibid., p. 71.   Ibid., p. 76.

34. Ibid., p. 98.   Ibid., p. 102.

35. Ibid., p. 125.   Ibid., p. 130.

36. Ibid., pp. 227-28.   Ibid., p. 235.

37. Ibid., p. 370.   Ibid., p. 378.

38. Lien, "Et annulert drap i Felicias bryllup." Om Sandemose -
en rapport fra Jante, pp. 128-30.

39. Verker i utvalg, VIII, p. 300.

40. Ibid., p. 302.

41. Ibid., p. 305. In legend a striking characteristic of the
werewolf is that its eyes always remain human.

42. Verker i utvalg, VIII, p. 305.

43. The Werewolf, p. 357.   Verker i utvalg, VII, p. 365.

44. Ibid.   Ibid.

45. Ibid.   Ibid.

46. Ibid.   Ibid.

47. Ibid., pp. 357-58.   Ibid., p. 366.

48. Ibid., p. 86.   Ibid., p. 91.

49. Ibid., p. 96.   Ibid., p. 100.

50. Ibid., p. 86.   Ibid., p. 90.

51. Ibid., p. 7.   Ibid., pp. 11-12.

52. Ibid., p. 96.   Ibid., p. 101.

53. Ibid., p. 26.   Ibid., p. 31.

54. Ibid., p. 222.   Ibid., p. 229.

55. Ibid., p. 223.   Ibid., p. 230.

56. Ibid., p. 325.   Ibid., p. 333.

57. Ibid., p. 26.   Ibid., p. 31.

11.

Conclusion

In spite of their apparent diversity, a close reading of
Sandemose's works reveals a striking cohesiveness. The same
anguished voice is speaking through the various narrators from
Tales from Labrador through The Werewolf and Felicia's Wedding.
Only towards the end of the author's life, after Sandemose had
abandoned fiction for good in favor of autobiography, did this
voice lose its bitter tone. The Walls around Jericho is the work
of a human being who has accepted his fate and is finally at peace
with the world. Before reaching this point, however, Sandemose's
narrators are desperately trying to understand their past and their
present, and hopefully perceive glimpses of what the future may
have in store. What is at the root of war and violence? What is
the relationship between warfare among nations and the little battles that individuals are constantly fighting with each other? Is
it possible either to sublimate our destructive energy or else turn
it into a positive force, which might be utilized to construct a
truly free, humane society? These are questions Sandemose's protagonists are constantly posing and which each of them answers in a
slightly different way.

Sandemose's characters possess a double nature; like satyrs or
werewolves they are part human, part animal. The author is constantly comparing them to horses, rats, dogs, wolves, bears, or
tigers. The wilder the animal, the more dangerous the association.
The animal element is not always negative. Vera in September was
compared to a young mare in her erotic encounter with Røde Fane,
and Felicia in The Werewolf was frequently given horse attributes
as well. The horse is a symbol of sexuality, which in Sandemose's
work may be seen as a positive, lifegiving force. More frequently,
however, the horse's qualities are looked upon in a negative way,

especially when they are permitted to dominate the individual.
They are particularly dangerous when coupled with physical
strength. The mating of the huge stallion and the tiny mare in A
Sailor goes Ashore is catastrophic, leading to the destruction of
both. The ideal sexual encounter takes place between two people
(horses) of equal physical strength, as is the case with Vera and
Røde Fane. Erling Vik in The Werewolf resents Felicia's sexuality
because it is too powerful for him. He fails to see that he is the
only person who would be able to tame Felicia's wild-horse qualities and by so doing assist her in becoming a harmonious human
being. Erling's fear of Felicia resembles Espen's fear of Kristine
in A Sailor Goes Ashore.

Nevertheless, the problem of an overpowering sexual drive is a
male problem in most of Sandemose's works. In his dreams Espen
Arnakke would frequently transform his father into a horse. As a
rule of thumb, however, Sandemose will generally compare his
females to horses, while his male characters are associated with
wolves or other even more dangerous animals. They are individuals
whose humanity has been suppressed by their animal qualities, and
who are difficult, if not impossible, to domesticate. It is interesting that Sandemose's "werewolves" are individuals who are
repressed and lack natural outlets for their erotic drives. The
Pastor in Horns for Our Adornment and Tor Anderssen in The Werewolf
are excellent examples. Females, of course, may suffer the same
fate. Gulnare, who had her natural instincts for love literally
beaten out of her system at the age of fourteen, becomes a werewolf
as well.

One significant reason for the misery of human beings in
general and the war between the sexes in particular is the male-
created myth of female purity. The idealization of woman as a
madonna creates a barrier against any attempt at healthy social
living. Yet the myth is so powerful that Erling Vik, even after
having had the opportunity to compare Felicia and Gulnare as
middle-aged women, continues to dream of and long for the innocent
young girl he lost at the age of sixteen.

Sandemose's characters have several ways of dealing with their
animal instincts. One is through insanity; this is, of course, an
extreme solution, as exemplified by the madwoman in Alice Atkinson
and Her Lovers. Most of Sandemose's protagonists choose a more
constructive solution. Gullhesten in Horns for Our Adornment recognized that, unleashed, the combination of his sexuality and physical force was a mortal danger to other people. He therefore sub-
limated his need to express his emotions erotically by carving the
statue of Gulnare, and by so doing neutralizing his desire for a
real woman. Gullhesten chose to become an artist, to "ride" the
winged Pegasus instead of a flesh-and-blood human being. This was
to be the choice as well of John Torson in The Past Is a Dream,
Jørgen Haukli in Alice Atkinson, and finally Erling Vik in The
Werewolf.

Nevertheless, between Gullhesten and Erling Vik considerable
progress has been made. The society Gullhesten creates eliminates
women altogether. In The Past Is a Dream and Alice Atkinson the
writing appears to serve the writer himself almost exclusively.
John Torson is totally enmeshed in his attempt to reconstruct the
past; the future does not concern him. Jørgen Haukli, on the other
hand, is deeply disturbed by the future, which he envisions as a
wasteland, a world which has lost its soul. Erling Vik alone is a
truly visionary artist, dedicating his work to exposing Felicia's
dream of an open, humane society, where people are free to form
natural relationships among one another without being restricted by
conventional morality.

The vision of the future perceived in The Werewolf is, to be
sure, a reaction against conventional twentieth-century society,
based as it is upon the spirit of competition and violence. It is
not, however, an invitation to return to nature. In Tales from
Labrador the Indian society appeared to function precisely because
its members respected a set of simple, practical rules, based upon
common sense. Obversely, the rules Espen Arnakke observed in Jante
were based upon pure stupidity. Moreover, they gave the individual
no guidance as to possible growth and expansion. They were
exclusively negative, instructing him in what he must not do.
Under such conditions, it was very tempting for an Audun Hamre to
curse the world and withdraw into his own self, or for a John
Torson and Jørgen Haukli to withdraw into art. Felicia, of course,
was far less cynical, but she too believed that left totally alone
people would grow in dangerous, unpredictable ways. Her Venhaug
was a carefully cultivated garden. She herself had chosen which
species would be admitted and which combinations would be most
likely to produce superior offspring. Nevertheless, even Felicia
could not prevent weeds from growing, and she did not have the psychological strength to get rid of them. In fact, it was a weakness
in Felicia herself, namely her unbridled eroticism, that stained
her Eden. The greenhouse she constructs is clearly related to
Abraham's field in A Sailor Goes Ashore, to Adamsen's barn in A
Fugitive Crosses His Tracks, and to Moen's orchard in Alice
Atkinson; all these places are related to erotic transgression.

It is interesting to notice, however, that while the field,
the barn, and the orchard were owned by powerful father figures,
Venhaug is Felicia's creation. While Jan is still the legitimate
owner of the farm, Felicia is wealthy in her own right and in every
way her husband's equal. More important, she is the visionary and
the spiritual center of the Venhaug society. Her guide, the old
gardener of her youth, was a mild-mannered, simple man who taught
by example rather than harsh words, scorn, punishment, or even
expulsion. What Sandemose appears to be telling us is that in the
society of the future androgyny rather than rigid sexual separation
must be the norm. The end of Jante marks the end of male rule.
While the old society was based on the tyranny of the strong over
the weak, of big brother over little brother, of man over woman,
the new society must be built upon the principle of equality and

individual expansion. This new society is not realized at Venhaug.
In fact, the perfect society can perhaps not be constructed in this
world because it is at odds with basic human cravings; unbridled
eroticism, greed, and violence are always placing human happiness
in jeopardy. Nevertheless, Felicia did possess the dream of a new
world. After her death Erling felt compelled to dig up his golden
hammer, that is his artistic talent, and dedicate it to the propa-
gation of Felicia's vision. Therefore, in spite of the fact that
the Venhaug experiment was at best a qualified success, the ending
of The Werewolf is optimistic. According to an earlier Sandemose
narrator: "All those who possess the dream of a purified humanity,
will awaken one day at the gate of heaven."

Selected Bibliography

Works by Aksel Sandemose

Fortællinger fra Labrador. Copenhagen: Gyldendal, 1923.

Storme ved Jævndøgn. Copenhagen: Gyldendal, 1924.

Ungdomssynd. Copenhagen: E. Jespersens Forlag, 1924.

Mænd fra Atlanteren. Copenhagen: Forlaget Af, 1924.

Klabavtermanden. Copenhagen: Gyldendal, 1927.

Ross Dane. Copenhagen: Gyldendal, 1928.

En sjømann går i land. Oslo: Gyldendal, 1931.

Klabautermannen. Oslo: Gyldendal, 1932.

En flyktning krysser sitt spor. Fortelling om en morders barndom. Oslo: Tiden, 1933.

Fesjå, 1-4. Oslo 1934-36.

Vi pynter oss med horn. Oslo: Tiden, 1936.

Sandemose forteller. Oslo: Tiden, 1937.

Der stod en benk i haven. Oslo: Tiden, 1937.

Brudulje. Oslo: Tiden, 1938.

September. Oslo: Tiden, 1939.

Fortellinger fra andre tider. Oslo: Aschehoug, 1940.

Det gångna är en dröm. Stockholm: Bonnier, 1944.

Tjærehandleren. Oslo: Aschehoug, 1945.

Det svundne er en drøm. Oslo: Aschehoug, 1946.

Alice Atkinson og hennes elskere. Oslo: Aschehoug, 1949.

Eventyret fra kong Rhascall den syttendes tid om en palmegrønn øy. Oslo: Aschehoug, 1950.

Årstidene, 1-13. Oslo 1951-55.

Reisen til Kjørkelvik. Copenhagen: Hans Reitzels Forlag, 1954.

En flyktning krysser sitt spor. Espen Arnakkes kommentarer til Janteloven. Kjørkelvik: A. Sandemose, 1955.

Varulven. Oslo: Aschehoug, 1958.

Murene rundt Jeriko. Oslo: Aschehoug, 1960.

Felicias bryllup. Oslo: Aschehoug, 1961.

Mytteriet på barken Zuidersee. Oslo: Aschehoug, 1963.

Verker i utvalg, vols. I-VIII. Oslo: Aschehoug, 1965-66.

Som et neshorn med hjernebetennelse, edited by Johannes Væth. Oslo: Aschehoug, 1972.

Dikteren og temaet, edited by Peter Larsen and Thorleif Skjævesland. Oslo: Aschehoug, 1973.

Epistler og moralske tanker, edited by Trygve Larsen. Oslo: Aschehoug, 1973.

Brev fra Kjørkelvik, edited by Petter Larsen and Thorleif Skjævesland. Oslo: Aschehoug, 1974.

Minner fra andre dager, edited by Petter Larsen and Thorleif Skjævesland. Oslo: Aschehoug, 1975.

Bakom står hin onde og hoster så smått, edited by Petter Larsen and Thorleif Skjævesland. Oslo: Aschehoug, 1976.

In English Translation

A Fugitive Crosses His Tracks, translated by Eugene Gay-Tifft.* New York: A. A. Knopf, 1936.

Horns for Our Adornment, translated by Eugene Gay-Tifft.* New
York: A. A. Knopf, 1938.

The Werewolf, translated by Gustaf Lannestock, with an
introduction by Harald S. Næss. Madison and Milwaukee: The
University of Wisconsin Press, 1966.

Mutiny on the Barque Zuidersee, translated by Maurice Michael.
London: Neville Spearman, 1970.

Biographical and Critical Studies

Alfredsson, Ulla. Språk, sexualitet, fascism, En studie in Aksel
Sandemoses roman Vi pynter oss med horn. Göteborg: Göteborgs
universitetet, Litteraturvetenskapliga institutionen, 1976.

Andersson, Lars. "Aksel Sandemose - pojken som såg varulven."
Folket i Bild 1976.

Anthi, Per. "Kriminalforfatteren Sandemose." Samtiden 1972.

Brenöe, Claus. "En kritisk analyse av Varulvens kronologi." Edda
1980.

Braatøy, Tryggve. "Kjærlighet og hat." Edda 1933.

Dahl, Willy. "Sandemose kladder en roman - men er heldigvis selv
med." Orientering 1961.

_____. "Morderpsykologi og hvetepriser. En revurdering av
Sandemose." Konfrontasjoner, edited by Willy Dahl and Knut
Johansen. Oslo: Ny Dag, 1970.

Eggen, Einar. "Jante." Syn og segn 1962.

_____. Espen Arnakke og hans verden, Bidrag til en analyse av
En flyktning krysser sitt spor. Oslo: Aschehoug, 1981.

Eidem, Odd. "En person søker ikke en forfatter." Goddag og adjø.
Oslo 1977.

Eldevik, Gunnvald. "Ensomhet og fellesskap. Om Sandemose - en
rapport fra Jante, edited by Johannes Væth. Nykøbing Mors:
Forfatterforlaget Attika, 1974.

Estvad, Leo. Aksel Sandemose først i 20'erne. Copenhagen: Carit
Andersens Forlag, 1967.

Gjesdal, Paul. "Edens have." Samtiden 1934.

Havnevik, Ivar. "Kjærlighet og verdi i Aksel Sandemoses roman
Varulven. Norskrift nr. 16. Oslo: Nordisk Institutt,
Universitetet i Oslo, Blindern 3, 1977.

Holmesland, Hilde. "'Konkurransen, sammenlikningen, er mannens
ulykke'." Edda 1980.

Houm, Philip. "En som ble til noe" (1965). Gleder og gremmelser.
Oslo 1977.

Haaland, Arild. "Flyktningen - Varulven tur - retur. En linje i
Sandemoses diktning." Vinduet 1965.

Kallström, Moni. "Mænd fra Atlanteren - Malstrøm." Om Sandemose
- en rapport fra Jante, edited by Johannes Væth. Nykøbing Mors:
Forfatterforlaget Attika, 1967.

Larsen, Petter. "En morders barndom. En litteratur-psykologisk
analyse av Sandemoses Espen Arnakke-skikkelse." Vinduet 1962.

Larsen, Petter. Sandemose. Norske forfattere i nærlys. Oslo:
Aschehoug, 1972.

Lien, Asmund. "Store John vender tilbake." Edda 1965.

_____. "Sin egen historiker - sin samtids historiker."
Sandemoses ansikter, edited by Niels Birger Wamberg. Oslo:
Aschehoug, 1969.

_____. "Hulemotivet hos Aksel Sandemose." Samtiden 1970.

_____. "Et annulert drap i Felicias bryllup." Om Sandemose -
en rapport fra Jante, edited by Johannes Væth. Nykøbing Mors:
Forfatterforlaget Attika, 1974.

Nielsen, Frederik. "Varulven." Sandemoses ansikter, edited by
Niels Birger Wamberg. Oslo: Aschehoug, 1969.

Nielsen, Hans Jørgen, "Arbejderforfatteren Sandemose og
arbejderismens overvindelse. Hastige bemærkninger efter en
genlæsning." Vinduet 1979.

Nissen, Torben Ulrik. "Alice Atkinson og hennes elskere." Om
Sandemose - en rapport fra Jante, edited by Johannes Væth.
Nykøbing Mors: Forfatterforlaget Attika, 1974.

Nordberg, Carl-Eric. Sandemose. En biografi, translated by
Petter Larsen. Oslo: Aschehoug, 1967.

Sandemose, Pia. "Bonden og byen." Om Sandemose - en rapport fra
Jante, edited by Johannes Væth. Nykøbing Mors: Forfatterforlaget
Attika, 1974.

Schjelderup, Alv G. "Aksel Sandemose." Samtiden 1937.

Skjævesland, Torleif. "Aksel Sandemose og politikken." Samtiden 1973.

_____. "To forfattere i kontakt og konflikt. Aksel Sandemose og Arnulf Øverland." Samtiden 1974.

Soland, Jostein. "Kjærlighetsrittet i Varulven." Om Sandemose - en rapport fra Jante, edited by Johannes Væth. Nykøbing Mors: Forfatterforlaget Attika, 1974.

Storstein, Olav. "Aksel Sandemose, Jante og Den flyvende hollender." Fra Jæger til Falk. Oslo: Tiden, 1950.

Ustvedt, Yngvar. "Mytedikteren Aksel Sandemose." Samtiden 1966.

Vesaas, Tarjei. "Ein ubevisst trekkfugl." Sandemoses ansikter, edited by Niels Birger Wamberg. Oslo: Aschehoug, 1969.

Vogt, Johan. Aksel Sandemose. Minner, brev, betraktninger. Oslo: Aschehoug, 1973.

Væth, Johannes and Frits Johannesen. Aksel Sandemose og Danmark. Oslo: Aschehoug, 1963.

_____. Aksel Sandemose og Skandinavia. En bibliografi. Oslo: Aschehoug, 1969.

Væth, Johannes. Aksel Sandemose og Jante. Oslo: Aschehoug, 1966.

_____, editor. Om Sandemose - en rapport fra Jante. Nykøbing Mors: Forfatterforlaget Attika, 1974.

_____. På sporet af Sandemose. Nykøbing Mors: Forfatterforlaget Attika, 1975.

_____. Nykøbing Mors og Jante. Nykøbing Mors, Frisø, 1979.

Wamberg, Niels Birger, editor. Sandemoses ansikter. Oslo: Aschehoug, 1969.

Aarbakke, Jorunn Hareide. "En dikter krysser sitt spor. En strukturell og tematisk sammenlikning mellom Klabautermanden og Klabautermannen av Aksel Sandemose." Edda 1969.

_____. "Den første kjærligheten i Vi pynter oss med horn." Tekstopplevelser, edited by Willy Dahl. Oslo: Universitetsforlaget, 1970.

_____. "Sandemose i 30-årene. Drøm og diktning." Om Sandemose - en rapport fra Jante, edited by Johannes Væth. Nykøbing Mors: Forfatterforlaget Attika, 1974.

_____. "Dumhetens opprør. Aksel Sandemose og nazismen." Nazisme og norsk litteratur, edited by Bjarte Birkeland and Stein Uglevik Larsen. Bergen, Oslo, Tromsø: Universitetsforlaget, 1975.

_____. Høyt på en vinget hest. Oslo: Aschehoug, 1976.

_____. "Doktordisputas på avhandlingen Høyt på en vinget hest." Edda 1980.

*I have not used the translations of Gay-Tifft because they were not available in the University of Oregon library.

Index

ABOUT THE AUTHOR

Randi Birn was born in Tromsø, Norway. She received a cand.
philol. from the University of Oslo in 1960, wrote her doctoral
dissertation on Marcel Proust, and was awarded a Ph.D. by the
University of Illinois in 1965. At present Randi Birn is Professor
of French at the University of Oregon, where she has taught since
1965. Professor Birn is the author of Johan Borgen (Twayne, 1974).
An expanded version of this book was translated into Norwegian and
published under the title Johan Borgen. En litterær biografi
(Oslo: Gyldendal, 1977). She is the coeditor of Orion Blinded:
Essays on Claude Simon (Lewisburg: Bucknell University Press,
1981). Professor Birn has published a number of articles on modern
writers such as Proust, Simon, Genêt, Claudel, and Borgen. She is
currently doing research on modern French women writers.